∿ *To Bless the Space Between Us*

ALSO BY JOHN O'DONOHUE

Beauty: The Invisible Embrace

Anam Cara: A Book of Celtic Wisdom

Eternal Echoes: Celtic Reflections on Our Yearning to Belong

Conamara Blues: Poems

Divine Beauty

To Bless

THE SPACE BETWEEN US

A Book of Blessings

JOHN O'DONOHUE

DOUBLEDAY

NEW YORK LONDON TORONTO

SYDNEY AUCKLAND

PUBLISHED BY DOUBLEDAY

Copyright © 2008 by John O'Donohue

All Rights Reserved

Published in the United States by Doubleday, an imprint of
The Doubleday Broadway Publishing Group, a division of
Random House, Inc., New York.
www.doubleday.com

DOUBLEDAY and the portrayal of an anchor with a dolphin
are registered trademarks of Random House, Inc.

Library of Congress Cataloging-in-Publication Data
O'Donohue, John, 1956–
  To bless the space between us : a book of blessings /
John O'Donohue.
     p. cm.
1. Prayers. 2. Benedictions. I. Title.
  BV245.O33 2008
  242'.8—dc22
                                        2007031558

ISBN 978-0-385-52227-4

PRINTED IN THE UNITED STATES OF AMERICA

19

FIRST EDITION

~ FOR OLIVIA LEONARD,

Soul to soul
Through all the years

Contents

∿ *To Bless the Space Between Us*

Introduction

There is a quiet light that shines in every heart. It draws no attention to itself, though it is always secretly there. It is what illuminates our minds to see beauty, our desire to seek possibility, and our hearts to love life. Without this subtle quickening our days would be empty and wearisome, and no horizon would ever awaken our longing. Our passion for life is quietly sustained from somewhere in us that is wedded to the energy and excitement of life. This shy inner light is what enables us to recognize and receive our very presence here as blessing. We enter the world as strangers who all at once become heirs to a harvest of memory, spirit, and dream that has long preceded us and will now enfold, nourish, and sustain us. The gift of the world is our first blessing.

It would be infinitely lonely to live in a world without blessing. The word *blessing* evokes a sense of warmth and protection; it suggests that no life is alone or unreachable. Each life is clothed in raiment of spirit that secretly links it to everything else. Though suffering and chaos befall us, they can never quench that inner light of providence.

While our culture is all gloss and pace on the outside, within it is too often haunted and lost. The commercial edge of so-called "progress" has cut away a huge region of human tissue and webbing that held us in communion with one another. We have fallen out of belonging. Consequently, when we stand before crucial thresholds in our lives, we have no rituals to protect, encourage, and guide us as we cross over into the unknown. For such crossings we need to find new words. What is nearest to the heart is often farthest from the word. This book is an attempt to reach into that tenuous territory of change that we must traverse when a threshold invites us. Each blessing is intended to present a minimal psychic portrait of the geography of change it names. Without warning, thresholds can open directly before our feet. These thresholds are also the shorelines of new worlds. The blessings here attempt to offer a brief geography of the new experience and some pathways of presence through it.

It has been a daunting undertaking over several years to create these blessings. A blessing evokes a privileged intimacy. It touches that tender membrane where the human heart cries out to its divine ground. In the ecstasy and loneliness of one's life, there are certain times when blessing is nearer to us than any other person or thing. A blessing is not a sentiment or a question; it is a gracious invocation where the human heart pleads with the divine heart. There is nothing more intimate in a life than the secret underterritory where it anchors. Regardless of our differences in religion, language, or concept, there is no heart that is without this inner divine reference. It is the modest wish of this book to illuminate the gift that a blessing can be, the doors it can open, the healing and transfiguration it can bring. Our times are desperate for meaning and belonging.

In the parched deserts of postmodernity a blessing can be like the discovery of a fresh well. It would be lovely if we could rediscover our power to bless one another. I believe each of us can bless. When a blessing is invoked, it changes the atmosphere. Some of the plenitude flows into our hearts from the invisible neighborhood of loving kindness. In the light and reverence of blessing, a person or situation becomes illuminated in a completely new way. In a dead wall a new window opens, in dense darkness a path starts to glimmer, and into a broken heart healing falls like morning dew. It is ironic that so often we continue to live like paupers though our inheritance of spirit is so vast. The quiet eternal that dwells in our souls is silent and subtle; in the activity of blessing it emerges to embrace and nurture us. Let us begin to learn how to bless one another. Whenever you give a blessing, a blessing returns to enfold you.

A blessing is a difficult form to render. I have endeavored to write them as poetically as possible, but they are not poems. A poem is an utterly independent linguistic object. It begins with its first syllable and ends with the last; in between it is its own force field. In contrast, the blessing form has an eye to the outside in order to embrace and elevate whatever is happening to someone. It is direct address, driven by immediacy and care. A poem is inevitably more oblique; it works deep underneath conversation.

This sequence of blessings follows seven rhythms of the human journey: beginnings, desires, thresholds, homecomings, states of the heart, callings, and beyond endings. The temptation in writing blessings is to employ the word *God* at every juncture. I have chosen not to do this. First, it would be utterly repetitive; second, the word *God* is too huge to allow any other word to breathe beside it. Furthermore, it is unnecessary; God is omnipresent, and life itself is the primal sacrament, namely, *the* visible sign of invisible grace. The structures of our experience are the windows into the divine. When we are true to the call of experience, we are true to God.

The language of blessing is invocation, a calling forth. This is why the word *may* occurs throughout the book; it is a word of benediction. It imagines and wills the fulfillment of desire. In the evocation of our blessings here, the word *may* is the spring through which the Holy Spirit is invoked to surge into presence and effect. The Holy Spirit is the subtle presence and secret energy behind every blessing here.

Each person has a unique intimacy with God. I have kept these blessing forms open and not particularized their divine source; for me personally, when I bless, I do it in the name and spirit of Jesus. At the end of the book I include a poetic evocation of the infinite kindness in his gaze. The book concludes with a poetic essay on recovering the lost art of blessing; here I explore what blessing is, where it meets us, and how the Celtic imagination framed so much of life in blessing.

May we all receive blessing upon blessing. And may we realize our power to bless, heal, and renew one another.

There are days when Conamara is wreathed in blue Tuscan light. The mountains seem to waver as though they were huge dark ships on a distant voyage. I love to climb up into the silence of these vast autonomous structures. What seems like a pinnacled summit from beneath becomes a level plateau when you arrive there. Born in a red explosion of ascending fire, the granite lies cold, barely marked by the millions of years of rain and wind. On this primeval ground I feel I have entered into a pristine permanence, a continuity here that knew the wind hundreds of millions of years before a human face ever felt it.

When we arrive into the world, we enter this ancient sequence. All our beginnings happen within this continuity. Beginnings often frighten us because they seem like lonely voyages into the unknown. Yet, in truth, no beginning is empty or isolated. We seem to think that beginning is setting out from a lonely point along some line of direction into the unknown. This is not the case. Shelter and energy come alive when a beginning is embraced. Goethe says that once the commitment is made, destiny conspires with us to support and realize it. We are never as alone in our beginnings as it might seem at the time. A beginning is ultimately an invitation to open toward the gifts and growth that are stored up for us. To refuse to begin can be an act of great self-neglect.

Perhaps beginnings make us anxious because we did not begin ourselves. Others began us. Being conceived and born, we eventually enter upon ourselves already begun, already there. Instinctively we grasp onto and continue within the continuity in which we find ourselves. Indeed, our very life here depends directly on continuous acts of beginning. But these beginnings are out of our hands; they decide themselves. This is true of our breathing and our heartbeat. Beginning precedes us, creates us, and constantly takes us to new levels and places and people. There is nothing to fear in the act of beginning. More often than not it knows the journey ahead better than we ever could. Perhaps the art of harvesting the secret riches of our lives is best achieved when we place profound trust in the act of beginning. Risk might be our greatest ally. To live a truly creative life, we always need to cast a critical look at where we presently are, attempting always to discern where we have become stagnant and where new beginning might be ripening. There can be no growth if we do not remain open and vulnerable to what is new and different. I have never seen anyone take a risk for growth that was not rewarded a thousand times over.

There is a certain innocence about beginning, with its excitement and promise of something new. But this will emerge only through undertaking some voyage into the unknown. And no one can foretell what the unknown might yield. There are journeys we have begun that have brought us great inner riches and refinement; but we had to travel through dark valleys of difficulty and suffering. Had we known at the beginning what the journey would demand of us, we might never have set out. Yet the rewards and gifts became vital to who we are. Through the innocence of beginning we are often seduced into growth.

Sometimes the greatest challenge is to actually begin; there is something deep in us that conspires with what wants to remain within safe boundaries and stay the same. Years ago my neighbor here set out to build his new home. He had just stripped the sod off the field to begin digging out the foundation when an old man from the village happened to come by. He blessed the work and said, "You have the worst of it behind you now." My neighbor laughed and said, "But I have only just begun." The old man said, "That's what I mean. You have begun; and to make a real beginning is the most difficult act." There is an old Irish proverb that says, *"Tus maith leath na hoibre."* "A good beginning is half the work." There seems to be a wisdom here, when one considers all the considerations, hesitation, and uncertainty that can claim our hearts for such a long time before the actual act of beginning happens. Sometimes a period of preparation is necessary, where the idea of the beginning can gestate and refine itself; yet quite often we unnecessarily postpone and equivocate when we should simply take the risk and leap into a new beginning.

The Greeks believed that time had secret structure. There was the moment of Epiphany when time suddenly opened and something was revealed in luminous clarity. There was the moment of *krisis* when time got entangled and directions became confused and contradictory. There was also the moment of *kairos*; this was the propitious moment. Time opened up in kindness and promise. All the energies cohered to offer a fecund occasion of initiative, creativity, and promise. Part of the art of living wisely is to learn to recognize and attend to such profound openings in one's life. In the letters between Boris Pasternak and Olga Ivinskaya there is the beautiful recognition: "When a great moment knocks on the door of your life, its sound is often no louder than the beating of your heart and it is very easy to miss it." To live a conscious life, we need to constantly refine our listening.

The Jewish tradition believed that time had its own psychic seasons. In the book of Ecclesiastes there is a list of the correspondences between certain events and their proper time:

> *To every thing, there is a season, and a time to every purpose under the heaven:*
> *A time to be born, and a time to die; a time to plant, and a time to pluck up that which is planted;*
> *A time to kill, and a time to heal; a time to break down, and a time to build up;*
> *A time to weep, and a time to laugh; a time to mourn, and a time to dance;*
> *A time to cast away stones, and a time to gather stones together; a time to embrace, and a time to refrain from embracing;*
> *A time to get, and a time to lose; a time to keep, and a time to cast away;*

A time to rend, and a time to sew; a time to keep silence, and
a time to speak;
A time to love, and a time to hate; a time of war, and a time
of peace.

Before it occurs, a beginning can be a long time in preparation. This is why some beginnings take off with great assuredness, and one can instinctively recognize that the right direction has been chosen. Without any struggle, one enters into a fluency that seemed to have been awaiting one's choice. Other beginnings are awkward and slow, and it takes considerable time before the new path opens or welcomes one. Sometimes beginnings can catch us unawares. Often when something is ending we discover within it the spore of new beginning, and a whole new train of possibility is in motion before we even realize it.

When the heart is ready for a fresh beginning, unforeseen things can emerge. And in a sense, this is exactly what a beginning does. It is an opening for surprises. Surrounding the intention and the act of beginning, there are always exciting possibilities. This inevitably excites artists. So much can actually happen between the moment the brush is taken into the hand and the moment it touches the canvas. Such beginnings have their own mind, and they invite and unveil new gifts and arrivals in one's life. Beginnings are new horizons that want to be seen; they are not regressions or repetitions. Somehow they win clearance and become fiercely free of the grip of the past. What is the new horizon in you that wants to be seen?

MATINS

1

Somewhere, out at the edges, the night
Is turning and the waves of darkness
Begin to brighten the shore of dawn

The heavy dark falls back to earth
And the freed air goes wild with light,
The heart fills with fresh, bright breath
And thoughts stir to give birth to color.

2

I arise today

In the name of Silence
Womb of the Word,
In the name of Stillness
Home of Belonging,
In the name of the Solitude
Of the Soul and the Earth.

I arise today

Blessed by all things,
Wings of breath,
Delight of eyes,
Wonder of whisper,
Intimacy of touch,
Eternity of soul,

Urgency of thought,
Miracle of health,
Embrace of God.

May I live this day

Compassionate of heart,
Clear in word,
Gracious in awareness,
Courageous in thought,
Generous in love.

A Morning Offering

I bless the night that nourished my heart
To set the ghosts of longing free
Into the flow and figure of dream
That went to harvest from the dark
Bread for the hunger no one sees.

All that is eternal in me
Welcomes the wonder of this day,
The field of brightness it creates
Offering time for each thing
To arise and illuminate.

I place on the altar of dawn:
The quiet loyalty of breath,
The tent of thought where I shelter,
Waves of desire I am shore to
And all beauty drawn to the eye.

May my mind come alive today
To the invisible geography
That invites me to new frontiers,
To break the dead shell of yesterdays,
To risk being disturbed and changed.

May I have the courage today
To live the life that I would love,
To postpone my dream no longer
But do at last what I came here for
And waste my heart on fear no more.

A BLESSING FOR THE NEW YEAR

BEANNACHT
For Josie.

On the day when
The weight deadens
On your shoulders
And you stumble,
May the clay dance
To balance you.

And when your eyes
Freeze behind
The gray window
And the ghost of loss
Gets into you,
May a flock of colors,
Indigo, red, green
And azure blue,
Come to awaken in you
A meadow of delight.

When the canvas frays
In the curragh of thought
And a stain of ocean
Blackens beneath you,
May there come across the waters
A path of yellow moonlight
To bring you safely home.

May the nourishment of the earth be yours,
May the clarity of light be yours,
May the fluency of the ocean be yours,
May the protection of the ancestors be yours.

And so may a slow
Wind work these words
Of love around you,
An invisible cloak
To mind your life.

Let us praise the grace and risk of Fire.

In the beginning,
The Word was red,
And the sound was thunder,
And the wound in the unseen
Spilled forth the red weather of being.

In the name of the Fire,
The Flame
And the Light:
Praise the pure presence of fire
That burns from within
Without thought of time.

The hunger of Fire has no need
For the reliquary of the future;
It adores the eros of now,
Where the memory of the earth
In flames that lick and drink the air
Is made to release

Its long-enduring forms
In a powder of ashes
Left for the wind to decipher.

As air intensifies the hunger of fire,
May the thought of death

Breathe new urgency
Into our love of life.

As fire cleanses dross,
May the flame of passion
Burn away what is false.

As short as the time
From spark to flame,
So brief may the distance be
Between heart and being.

May we discover
Beneath our fear
Embers of anger
To kindle justice.

May courage
Cause our lives to flame,
In the name of the Fire,
And the Flame
And the Light.

FOR A NEW BEGINNING

In out-of-the-way places of the heart,
Where your thoughts never think to wander,
This beginning has been quietly forming,
Waiting until you were ready to emerge.

For a long time it has watched your desire,
Feeling the emptiness growing inside you,
Noticing how you willed yourself on,
Still unable to leave what you had outgrown.

It watched you play with the seduction of safety
And the gray promises that sameness whispered,
Heard the waves of turmoil rise and relent,
Wondered would you always live like this.

Then the delight, when your courage kindled,
And out you stepped onto new ground,
Your eyes young again with energy and dream,
A path of plenitude opening before you.

Though your destination is not yet clear
You can trust the promise of this opening;
Unfurl yourself into the grace of beginning
That is at one with your life's desire.

Awaken your spirit to adventure;
Hold nothing back, learn to find ease in risk;
Soon you will be home in a new rhythm,
For your soul senses the world that awaits you.

Light cannot see inside things.
That is what the dark is for:
Minding the interior,
Nurturing the draw of growth
Through places where death
In its own way turns into life.

In the glare of neon times,
Let our eyes not be worn
By surfaces that shine
With hunger made attractive.

That our thoughts may be true light,
Finding their way into words
Which have the weight of shadow
To hold the layers of truth.

That we never place our trust
In minds claimed by empty light,
Where one-sided certainties
Are driven by false desire.

When we look into the heart,
May our eyes have the kindness
And reverence of candlelight.

That the searching of our minds
Be equal to the oblique

Crevices and corners where
The mystery continues to dwell,
glimmering in fugitive light.

When we are confined inside
The dark house of suffering
That moonlight might find a window.

When we become false and lost
That the severe noon-light
Would cast our shadow clear.

When we love, that dawn-light
Would lighten our feet
Upon the waters.

As we grow old, that twilight
Would illuminate treasure
In the fields of memory.

And when we come to search for God,
Let us first be robed in night,
Put on the mind of morning
To feel the rush of light
Spread slowly inside
The color and stillness
Of a found world.

May morning be astir with the harvest of night;
Your mind quickening to the eros of a new question,
Your eyes seduced by some unintended glimpse
That cut right through the surface to a source.

May this be a morning of innocent beginning,
When the gift within you slips clear
Of the sticky web of the personal
With its hurt and its hauntings,
And fixed fortress corners,

A morning when you become a pure vessel
For what wants to ascend from silence,

May your imagination know
The grace of perfect danger,

To reach beyond imitation,
And the wheel of repetition,

Deep into the call of all
The unfinished and unsolved

Until the veil of the unknown yields
And something original begins
To stir toward your senses
And grow stronger in your heart

In order to come to birth
In a clean line of form,
That claims from time
A rhythm not yet heard,
That calls space to
A different shape.

May it be its own force field
And dwell uniquely
Between the heart and the light

To surprise the hungry eye
By how deftly it fits
About its secret loss.

For a New Home

May this house shelter your life.
When you come in home here,
May all the weight of the world
Fall from your shoulders.

May your heart be tranquil here,
Blessed by peace the world cannot give.

May this home be a lucky place,
Where the graces your life desires
Always find the pathway to your door.

May nothing destructive
Ever cross your threshold.

May this be a safe place
Full of understanding and acceptance,
Where you can be as you are,
Without the need of any mask
Of pretense or image.

May this home be a place of discovery,
Where the possibilities that sleep
In the clay of your soul can emerge
To deepen and refine your vision
For all that is yet to come to birth.

May it be a house of courage,
Where healing and growth are loved,
Where dignity and forgiveness prevail;
A home where patience of spirit is prized,
And the sight of the destination is never lost
Though the journey be difficult and slow.
May there be great delight around this hearth.
May it be a house of welcome
For the broken and diminished.

May you have the eyes to see
That no visitor arrives without a gift
And no guest leaves without a blessing.

FOR A NEW POSITION

May your new work excite your heart,
Kindle in your mind a creativity
To journey beyond the old limits
Of all that has become wearisome.

May this work challenge you toward
New frontiers that will emerge
As you begin to approach them,
Calling forth from you the full force
And depth of your undiscovered gifts.

May the work fit the rhythms of your soul,
Enabling you to draw from the invisible
New ideas and a vision that will inspire.

Remember to be kind
To those who work for you,
Endeavor to remain aware
Of the quiet world
That lives behind each face.

Be fair in your expectations,
Compassionate in your criticism.
May you have the grace of encouragement
To awaken the gift in the other's heart,
Building in them the confidence
To follow the call of the gift.

May you come to know that work
Which emerges from the mind of love
Will have beauty and form.

May this new work be worthy
Of the energy of your heart
And the light of your thought.

May your work assume
A proper space in your life;
Instead of owning or using you,
May it challenge and refine you,
Bringing you every day further
Into the wonder of your heart.

There is great beauty in the notion of desire. Each of us is a child of the desire of our parents for each other. We are creatures of desire because we are creations of desire. The human heart discovers its most touching music when desire and love inform each other. When we love, we leave our separate solitudes and come toward union, where we complement each other. It is this ancient desire in every heart to discover and come home to its lost other half that awakens and activates its capacity for love and belonging. There are certain things that can happen to us only in solitude, and every life needs a rhythm of solitude in order to experience this. However, the experience of self-discovery, psychological integration, and spiritual growth can happen to us only when our desire draws us out of our shells and toward the precarious and life-giving sanctuary of another heart.

Desire is also at the heart of creativity. When we engage creatively, we depart from the fixed world of daily routine and grounded facts. We enter into a kind of "genesis foyer," where something that not yet is might begin to edge its way from silence into word, from the invisible into form. This is the excitement that fuels the writing life: the desire for what might emerge when the imagination begins to trawl the crowded seas of the white page. There is some pure desire in us to know what is original, to take leave of all the expected scripted perceptions that manipulate our experience. We long for an experience that is unfiltered, where the unknown could reach toward us without being filtered by us. For this reason the artistic life is vulnerable; it is often a chaotic and overwhelming place to attend. Yet when something true begins to emerge, it becomes the golden moment that redeems months of splintered time.

Desire is often expressed in restlessness. Nothing satisfies. This found classical modern expression in the Rolling Stones song "(I Can't Get No) Satisfaction." Ironically, this is probably the Augustinian rock song. Long before the Stones, Saint Augustine had said, "Thou hast made us for thyself, O Lord, and our hearts are restless until they find their rest in thee." Our dissatisfaction could, therefore, be the admission and awakening of our longing for the eternal. Rather than being simply the edge of some personal emptiness, it could be the first step in the opening up of our eternal belonging. In a much similar vein, Martin Heidegger once claimed that boredom might be the ideal predisposition for the mystical. The German word for *boredom* is *die Langeweile*, literally, "the long while." There is a certain irony in the realization that those who have succumbed to the utter indifference of boredom might find themselves already caught up in the most complex and challenging personal adventure: the mystical!

Our consumerist culture thrives on the awakening and manipulation of desire. This is how advertising works.

It stirs our desire and then cleverly directs it toward its products. Advertising is schooling in false desire; it relies on our need to belong, our need to play a central part in society, not exist on the fringes of it. Because awakened desire is full of immediacy, it wants gratification and does not want to be slowed down or wait. It wants no distance to open between it and the object of desire; it wants to have it now. This manipulation of desire accounts for the saturation of our culture with products that we don't need but are made to feel we do. There is no end to false desire. Like the consumption of fast food, it merely deepens and extends the hunger. It satisfies nothing in the end.

There is also a shadow side to desire; this is greed or addiction. When desire becomes blind to presence and becomes driven to have more and more, we have greed. It is as though some lonely infinite sleeps within desire, and when it comes awake it can destroy everything in its singular wish to possess. All perspective is lost, and vision is reduced to destructive ideology. This blind greed is at the heart of our environmental crisis.

In terms of its creative side, desire is the quickening of heart that calls forth change. Somehow the eye of desire can glimpse possibility where the overfamiliarized mind cannot see it. Once it glimpses this, desire cultivates dissatisfaction in the heart with what is, and kindles an impatience for that which has not yet emerged. Our dreams and fantasies showcase the directions in which our desire would love to lead us. Dreams are narratives of desire. We can learn the forms of longing within us, if we attend to our dreaming. There should always be a healthy tension between the life we have settled for and the desires that still call us. In this sense our desires are the messengers of our unlived life, calling us to attention and action while we still have time here to explore fields where the treasure dwells!

FOR EROS

When you love,
May you feel the joy
Of your heart coming alive
As your lover's gaze
Lands on your eyes,
Holding them,
Like the weight of a kiss,
Deepening.

May the words of love
Reach you and fluster
Your held self,
The way a silhouette of breeze
Excites a meadow.

When you are touched,
May it be the gentleness
You desire,
Your lover's hands sending
Each caress deep into your skin
Like a discovering glance.

May slow sequences
Of kisses discover
Your secret echoes.

May your desire flow free
And never be fettered

By the thorn-chains
Of old guilt
Or crippled touch.

May you feel
How your soul loves
When your skin glows,
And your eyes darken
When promise ripens.

In the gaze of your lover,
May you see clearer
In the mirror
Of your own being.

May the silences
Be spaces where you
Can gather swiftly,
At ease with all
The subtle complexity.

May you be able to listen
To your lover's heartbeat
And think only of the joy
You can awaken.

May you be able
To let yourself fall
Into the ocean rhythm,
Unfolding ever more

Until you become
One crest of wave,
Rising into wild foam

Whose beauty will show
In the graceful sweep
Of its home-breaking.

FOR FREEDOM

As a bird soars high
In the free holding of the wind,
Clear of the certainty of ground,
Opening the imagination of wings
Into the grace of emptiness
To fulfill new voyagings,
May your life awaken
To the call of its freedom.

As the ocean absolves itself
Of the expectation of land,
Approaching only
In the form of waves
That fill and pleat and fall
With such gradual elegance
As to make of the limit
A sonorous threshold
Whose music echoes back along
The give and strain of memory,
Thus may your heart know the patience
That can draw infinity from limitation.

As the embrace of the earth
Welcomes all we call death,
Taking deep into itself
The tight solitude of a seed,
Allowing it time
To shed the grip of former form

And give way to a deeper generosity
That will one day send it forth,
A tree into springtime,
May all that holds you
Fall from its hungry ledge
Into the fecund surge of your heart.

When the gentleness between you hardens
And you fall out of your belonging with each other,
May the depths you have reached hold you still.

When no true word can be said, or heard,
And you mirror each other in the script of hurt,
When even the silence has become raw and torn,
May you hear again an echo of your first music.

When the weave of affection starts to unravel
And anger begins to sear the ground between you,
Before this weather of grief invites
The black seed of bitterness to find root,
May your souls come to kiss.

Now is the time for one of you to be gracious,
To allow a kindness beyond thought and hurt,
Reach out with sure hands
To take the chalice of your love,
And carry it carefully through this echoless waste
Until this winter pilgrimage leads you
Toward the gateway to spring.

A Blessing of Angels

May the Angels in their beauty bless you.
May they turn toward you streams of blessing.

May the Angel of Awakening stir your heart
To come alive to the eternal within you,
To all the invitations that quietly surround you.

May the Angel of Healing turn your wounds
Into sources of refreshment.

May the Angel of the Imagination enable you
To stand on the true thresholds,
At ease with your ambivalence
And drawn in new directions
Through the glow of your contradictions.

May the Angel of Compassion open your eyes
To the unseen suffering around you.

May the Angel of Wildness disturb the places
Where your life is domesticated and safe,
Take you to the territories of true otherness

Where all that is awkward in you
Can fall into its own rhythm.

May the Angel of Eros introduce you
To the beauty of your senses

To celebrate your inheritance
As a temple of the holy spirit.

May the Angel of Justice disturb you
To take the side of the poor and the wronged.

May the Angel of Encouragement confirm you
In worth and self-respect,
That you may live with the dignity
That presides in your soul.

May the Angel of Death arrive only
When your life is complete
And you have brought every given gift
To the threshold where its infinity can shine.

May all the Angels be your sheltering
And joyful guardians.

For Longing

Blessed be the longing that brought you here
And quickens your soul with wonder.

May you have the courage to listen to the voice of
     desire
That disturbs you when you have settled for some-
     thing safe.

May you have the wisdom to enter generously into
     your own unease
To discover the new direction your longing wants
     you to take.

May the forms of your belonging—in love, creativity,
     and friendship—
Be equal to the grandeur and the call of your soul.

May the one you long for long for you.

May your dreams gradually reveal the destination of
     your desire.

May a secret Providence guide your thought and
     nurture your feeling.

May your mind inhabit your life with the sureness
     with which your body inhabits the world.

May your heart never be haunted by ghost-
    structures of old damage.

May you come to accept your longing as divine
    urgency.

May you know the urgency with which God longs
    for you.

In Praise of Air

Let us bless the air,
Benefactor of breath,
Keeper of the fragile bridge
We breathe across.

Air waiting outside
The womb, to funnel
A first breath
That lets us begin
To be here,
Each moment
Drawn from
Its invisible stock.

Air: vast neighborhood
Of the invisible, where thought lives,
Entering, to arise in us as our own,
Enabling us to put faces on things
That would otherwise stay strange
And leave us homeless here.

Air, home of memory where
Our vanished days secretly gather,
Receiving every glance, word, and act
That fall from presence,
Taking all our unfolding in,
So that nothing is lost or forgotten.

Air: reservoir of the future
Out of which our days flow,
Ferrying their shadowed nights,
The invisible generosity,
That brings us future friends
And sometimes stones of sorrow
On which our minds refine.

Air along whose unseen path
Presence builds its quiet procession;
Sometimes in waves of sound,
Voices that can persuade
Every door of the heart;
Often in tides of music
That absolve the cut of time.

Air: source of the breath
That enables flowers to flourish,
And calls the dark, rooted trees
To ascend into blossom.

Air, perfect emptiness
For the mind of birds
To map with vanishings;
Womb of forms
That shapes embraces
To hold animal presence.

Air makes the distance kind,
Opening pathways for the eye

To reach the affections of things,
Yet never lets its invisible geography
Come anywhere near thought
Or the voyage-edges of the eye.

Air: kingdom of spirit
Where our departed dwell,
Nearer to us than ever,
Where the gods preside.

Let us bless the invigoration
Of clean, fresh air.

The gentleness of air
That holds and slows the rain,
Lets it fall down.

The shyness of air
That never shows its face.

The force of air
In wall after wall
Of straining wind.

In the name of the air,
The breeze,
And the wind,
May our souls
Stay in rhythm
With eternal
Breath.

FOR THE SENSES

May the touch of your skin
Register the beauty
Of the otherness
That surrounds you.

May your listening be attuned
To the deeper silence
Where sound is honed
To bring distance home.

May the fragrance
Of a breathing meadow
Refresh your heart
And remind you you are
A child of the earth.

And when you partake
Of food and drink,
May your taste quicken
To the gift and sweetness
That flows from the earth.

May your inner eye
See through the surfaces
And glean the real presence
Of everything that meets you.

May your soul beautify
The desire of your eyes
That you might glimpse
The infinity that hides
In the simple sights
That seem worn
To your usual eyes.

For Presence

Awaken to the mystery of being here
and enter the quiet immensity of your own presence.

Have joy and peace in the temple of your senses.

Receive encouragement when new frontiers beckon.

Respond to the call of your gift and the courage to
follow its path.

Let the flame of anger free you of all falsity.

May warmth of heart keep your presence aflame.

May anxiety never linger about you.

May your outer dignity mirror an inner dignity of
soul.

Take time to celebrate the quiet miracles that seek
no attention.

Be consoled in the secret symmetry of your soul.

May you experience each day as a sacred gift woven
around the heart of wonder.

FOR FRIENDSHIP

May you be blessed with good friends,
And learn to be a good friend to yourself,
Journeying to that place in your soul where
There is love, warmth, and feeling.
May this change you.

May it transfigure what is negative, distant,
Or cold within your heart.

May you be brought into real passion, kindness,
And belonging.

May you treasure your friends.
May you be good to them, be there for them
And receive all the challenges, truth, and light you
    need.

May you never be isolated but know the embrace
Of your anam cara.

May you listen to your longing to be free.

May the frames of your belonging be generous enough for your dreams.

May you arise each day with a voice of blessing whispering in your heart.

May you find a harmony between your soul and your life.

May the sanctuary of your soul never become haunted.

May you know the eternal longing that lives at the heart of time.

May there be kindness in your gaze when you look within.

May you never place walls between the light and yourself.

May you allow the wild beauty of the invisible world to gather you, mind you, and embrace you in belonging.

FOR ABSENCE

May you know that absence is alive with hidden
    presence, that nothing is ever lost or forgotten.

May the absences in your life grow full of eternal
    echo.

May you sense around you the secret Elsewhere
    where the presences that have left you dwell.

May you be generous in your embrace of loss.

May the sore well of grief turn into a seamless flow
    of presence.

May your compassion reach out to the ones we never
    hear from.

May you have the courage to speak for the excluded
    ones.

May you become the gracious and passionate sub-
    ject of your own life.

May you not disrespect your mystery through brittle
    words or false belonging.

May you be embraced by God in whom dawn and
　　twilight are one.

May your longing inhabit its dreams within the
　　Great Belonging.

3 ◆ Thresholds

Within the grip of winter, it is almost impossible to imagine the spring. The gray perished landscape is shorn of color. Only bleakness meets the eye; everything seems severe and edged. Winter is the oldest season; it has some quality of the absolute. Yet beneath the surface of winter, the miracle of spring is already in preparation; the cold is relenting; seeds are wakening up. Colors are beginning to imagine how they will return. Then, imperceptibly, somewhere one bud opens and the symphony of renewal is no longer reversible. From the black heart of winter a miraculous, breathing plenitude of color emerges.

The beauty of nature insists on taking its time. Everything is prepared. Nothing is rushed. The rhythm of emergence is a gradual slow beat always inching its way forward; change remains faithful to itself until the new unfolds in the full confidence of true arrival. Because nothing is abrupt, the beginning of spring nearly always catches us unawares. It is there before we see it; and then we can look nowhere without seeing it.

Change arrives in nature when time has ripened. There are no jagged transitions or crude discontinuities. This accounts for the sureness with which one season succeeds another. It is as though they were moving forward in a rhythm set from within a continuum.

To change is one of the great dreams of every heart—to change the limitations, the sameness, the banality, or the pain. So often we look back on patterns of behavior, the kind of decisions we make repeatedly and that have failed to serve us well, and we aim for a new and more successful path or way of living. But change is difficult for us. So often we opt to continue the old pattern, rather than risking the danger of difference. We are also often surprised by change that seems to arrive out of nowhere. We find ourselves crossing some new threshold we had never anticipated. Like spring secretly at work within the heart of winter, below the surface of our lives huge changes are in fermentation. We never suspect a thing. Then when the grip of some long-enduring winter mentality begins to loosen, we find ourselves vulnerable to a flourish of possibility and we are suddenly negotiating the challenge of a threshold.

At any time you can ask yourself: At which threshold am I now standing? At this time in my life, what am I leaving? Where am I about to enter? What is preventing me from crossing my next threshold? What gift would enable me to do it? A threshold is not a simple boundary; it is a frontier that divides two different territories, rhythms, and atmospheres. Indeed, it is a lovely testimony to the fullness and integrity of an experience or a stage of life that it intensifies toward the end into a real frontier that cannot be crossed without the heart being passionately engaged and woken up. At this threshold a great complexity of emotion comes alive: confusion, fear, excitement, sadness, hope. This is one of the reasons such vital crossings were always clothed in ritual. It is wise in your own life to be able to recognize and acknowledge the key thresholds: to take your time; to feel all the varieties of presence that accrue there; to listen inward with complete attention until you hear the inner voice calling you forward. The time has come to cross.

To acknowledge and cross a new threshold is always a challenge. It demands courage and also a sense of trust in whatever is emerging. This becomes essential when a threshold opens suddenly in front of you, one for which you had no preparation. This could be illness, suffering, or loss. Because we are so engaged with the world, we usually forget how fragile life can be and how vulnerable we always are. It takes only a couple of seconds for a life to change irreversibly. Suddenly you stand on completely strange ground and a new course of life has to be embraced. Especially at such times we desperately need blessing and protection. You look back at the life you have lived up to a few hours before, and it suddenly seems so far away. Think for a moment how, across the world, someone's life has just changed—irrevocably, permanently, and not necessarily for the better—and everything that was once so steady, so reliable, must now find a new way of unfolding.

Though we know one another's names and recognize one another's faces, we never know what destiny shapes each life. The script of individual destiny is secret; it is hidden behind and beneath the sequence of happenings that is continually unfolding for us. Each life is a mystery that is never finally available to the mind's light or questions. That we are here is a huge affirmation; somehow life needed us and wanted us to be. To sense and trust this primeval acceptance can open a vast spring of trust within the heart. It can free us into a natural courage that casts out fear and opens up our lives to become voyages of discovery, creativity, and compassion. No threshold need be a threat, but rather an invitation and a promise. Whatever comes, the great sacrament of life will remain faithful to us, blessing us always with visible signs of invisible grace. We merely need to trust.

FOR YOUR BIRTHDAY

Blessed be the mind that dreamed the day
The blueprint of your life
Would begin to glow on earth,
Illuminating all the faces and voices
That would arrive to invite
Your soul to growth.

Praised be your father and mother,
Who loved you before you were,
And trusted to call you here
With no idea who you would be.

Blessed be those who have loved you
Into becoming who you were meant to be,
Blessed be those who have crossed your life
With dark gifts of hurt and loss
That have helped to school your mind
In the art of disappointment.

When desolation surrounded you,
Blessed be those who looked for you
And found you, their kind hands
Urgent to open a blue window
In the gray wall formed around you.

Blessed be the gifts you never notice,
Your health, eyes to behold the world,
Thoughts to countenance the unknown,

Memory to harvest vanished days,
Your heart to feel the world's waves,
Your breath to breathe the nourishment
Of distance made intimate by earth.

On this echoing-day of your birth,
May you open the gift of solitude
In order to receive your soul;
Enter the generosity of silence
To hear your hidden heart;
Know the serenity of stillness
To be enfolded anew
By the miracle of your being.

For the Traveler

Every time you leave home,
Another road takes you
Into a world you were never in.

New strangers on other paths await.
New places that have never seen you
Will startle a little at your entry.
Old places that know you well
Will pretend nothing
Changed since your last visit.

When you travel, you find yourself
Alone in a different way,
More attentive now
To the self you bring along,
Your more subtle eye watching
You abroad; and how what meets you
Touches that part of the heart
That lies low at home:

How you unexpectedly attune
To the timbre in some voice,
Opening a conversation
You want to take in
To where your longing
Has pressed hard enough
Inward, on some unsaid dark,
To create a crystal of insight

You could not have known
You needed
To illuminate
Your way.

When you travel,
A new silence
Goes with you,
And if you listen,
You will hear
What your heart would
Love to say.

A journey can become a sacred thing:
Make sure, before you go,
To take the time
To bless your going forth,
To free your heart of ballast
So that the compass of your soul
Might direct you toward
The territories of spirit
Where you will discover
More of your hidden life,
And the urgencies
That deserve to claim you.

May you travel in an awakened way,
Gathered wisely into your inner ground;
That you may not waste the invitations
Which wait along the way to transform you.

May you travel safely, arrive refreshed,
And live your time away to its fullest;
Return home more enriched, and free
To balance the gift of days which call you.

For a Mother-to-Be

Nothing could have prepared
Your heart to open like this.

From beyond the skies and the stars
This echo arrived inside you
And started to pulse with life,
Each beat a tiny act of growth,
Traversing all our ancient shapes
On its way home to itself.

Once it began, you were no longer your own.
A new, more courageous you, offering itself
In a new way to a presence you can sense
But you have not seen or known.

It has made you feel alone
In a way you never knew before;
Everyone else sees only from the outside
What you feel and feed
With every fiber of your being.

Never have you traveled farther inward
Where words and thoughts become half-light
Unable to reach the fund of brightness
Strengthening inside the night of your womb.

Like some primeval moon,
Your soul brightens

The tides of essence
That flow to your child.

You know your life has changed forever,
For in all the days and years to come,
Distance will never be able to cut you off
From the one you now carry
For nine months under your heart.

May you be blessed with quiet confidence
That destiny will guide you and mind you.

May the emerging spirit of your child
Imbibe encouragement and joy
From the continuous music of your heart,
So that it can grow with ease,
Expectant of wonder and welcome
When its form is fully filled

And it makes its journey out
To see you and settle at last
Relieved, and glad in your arms.

FOR A NEW FATHER

As the shimmer of dawn transforms the night
Into a blush of color futured with delight,
The eyes of your new child awaken in you
A brightness that surprises your life.

Since the first stir of its secret becoming,
The echo of your child has lived inside you,
Strengthening through all its night of forming
Into a sure pulse of fostering music.

How quietly and gently that embryo-echo
Can womb in the bone of a man
And foster across the distance to the mother
A shadow-shelter around this fragile voyage.

Now as you behold your infant, you know
That this child has come from you and to you;
You feel the full force of a father's desire
To protect and shelter.

Perhaps for the first time,
There awakens in you
A sense of your own mortality.

May your heart rest in the grace of the gift
And you sense how you have been called
Inside the dream of this new destiny.

May you be gentle and loving,
Clear and sure.

May you trust in the unseen providence
That has chosen you all to be a family.

May you stand sure on your ground
And know that every grace you need
Will unfold before you
Like all the mornings of your life.

Now is the time of dark invitation
Beyond a frontier you did not expect;
Abruptly, your old life seems distant.

You barely noticed how each day opened
A path through fields never questioned,
Yet expected, deep down, to hold treasure.
Now your time on earth becomes full of threat;
Before your eyes your future shrinks.

You lived absorbed in the day-to-day,
So continuous with everything around you,
That you could forget you were separate;

Now this dark companion has come between you.
Distances have opened in your eyes.
You feel that against your will
A stranger has married your heart.

Nothing before has made you
Feel so isolated and lost.

When the reverberations of shock subside in you,
May grace come to restore you to balance.
May it shape a new space in your heart
To embrace this illness as a teacher
Who has come to open your life to new worlds.

May you find in yourself
A courageous hospitality
Toward what is difficult,
Painful, and unknown.

May you learn to use this illness
As a lantern to illuminate
The new qualities that will emerge in you.

May the fragile harvesting of this slow light
Help to release whatever has become false in you.
May you trust this light to clear a path
Through all the fog of old unease and anxiety
Until you feel arising within you a tranquillity
Profound enough to call the storm to stillness.

May you find the wisdom to listen to your illness:
Ask it why it came. Why it chose your friendship.
Where it wants to take you. What it wants you to
     know.
What quality of space it wants to create in you.
What you need to learn to become more fully
     yourself
That your presence may shine in the world.

May you keep faith with your body,
Learning to see it as a holy sanctuary
Which can bring this night-wound gradually
Toward the healing and freedom of dawn.

May you be granted the courage and vision
To work through passivity and self-pity,
To see the beauty you can harvest
From the riches of this dark invitation.

May you learn to receive it graciously,
And promise to learn swiftly
That it may leave you newborn,
Willing to dedicate your time to birth.

At the Threshold of Womanhood

It is like awakening into a morning
Where everything is touched with change.
Now your body has a mind of its own
As it curves and fills into womanhood.

The lightness of being a girl is leaving,
And your thoughts too are taking you
To places you have never known before.

 Becoming a woman, you feel the moon
Tug at your blood, and you begin to sense
The mysteries of your new body.

May you enter beautifully into the feminine,
Learning to trust the world of feeling you inherit,
Finding ease and elegance in all you are.

May your respect for your beauty
Become visible in your dignity
And how you hold yourself in the world.

May the expectation in other eyes
Never decide how you are to be;
Learn to trust the advice of your heart.

May you feel life as an irresistible invitation
To discover and develop your talents,
Each day bringing something new to birth.

May you be wise in choosing love;
When you trust, give all your heart
And allow love to pervade you like breath.

May you have friends who can see you.
May your senses be windows of wonder
And your mind a prism of spirit.

As you leave the blurred wood
You entered while still a boy,
And light clarifies around
Your emerging, manly form,
May you discover gradually
A natural confidence in your body.

May your new strength be graceful
As you learn to carry yourself
With a dignity that is sure,
Bringing your gestures and expression
Into an easy harmony and rhythm.

May you never feel the need
To be coarse, or force yourself;
Rather, may you receive your manhood
With grace and mindful ease;
Then, at one with your own elegance,
Your presence will claim its radiance.

May you awaken confidently
To the feminine within you,
And learn to integrate the beauty
Of intuition and feeling
So that your sensitivity kindles
And your heart is trusted.

That you may slowly grow
To trust the silence of the masculine
As the home of your stillness.

Though it will be always difficult
To find the words for what you feel,
May you find ease in that awkwardness
Until gradually from beneath
The gravel of stuttered sounds
The pure flow of you emerges.

Be gentle with yourself,
Learn to integrate the negative,
Harnessing its force
To cross the boundaries
That would confine you.

Love the life of your mind,
Furnishing it ever with new thought
So that your countenance glows
With the joy of being alive.

Be vigilant
And true to an inner honor
That will not allow
Anger or resentment
To make you captive.

Always have the courage
To change, welcoming those voices
That call you beyond yourself.

Beyond your work and action,
Remain faithful to your heart,
For you to deepen and grow
Into a man of dignity and nobility.

FOR THE PARENTS OF ONE
WHO HAS COMMITTED A CRIME

No one else can see beauty
In his darkened life now.
His image has closed
Like a shadow.

When people look at him,
He has become the mirror
Of the damage he has done.

But he is yours;
And you have different eyes
That hold his yesterdays
In pictures no one else remembers:

Waiting for him to be born,
Not knowing who he would be,
The moments of his childhood,
First steps, first words,
Smiles and cries,
And all the big thresholds
Of his journey since . . .

He is yours in a way
No words could ever tell;
And you can see through
The stranger this deed has made him
And still find the countenance of your son.

Despite all the disappointment and shame,
May you find in your belonging with him
A kind place, where your spirit will find rest.
May new words come alive between you
To build small bridges of understanding.

May that serenity lead you beyond guilt and blame
To find that bright field of the heart
Where he can come to feel your love

Until it heals whatever darkness drove him
And he can see what it is he has done
And seek forgiveness and bring healing;
May this dark door open a path
That brightens constantly with new promise.

For a Parent on the Death of a Child

No one knows the wonder
Your child awoke in you,
Your heart a perfect cradle
To hold its presence.
Inside and outside became one
As new waves of love
Kept surprising your soul.

Now you sit bereft
Inside a nightmare,
Your eyes numbed
By the sight of a grave
No parent should ever see.

You will wear this absence
Like a secret locket,
Always wondering why
Such a new soul
Was taken home so soon.

Let the silent tears flow
And when your eyes clear
Perhaps you will glimpse
How your eternal child
Has become the unseen angel
Who parents your heart
And persuades the moon
To send new gifts ashore.

For Old Age

May the light of your soul mind you.

May all your worry and anxiousness about your age
Be transfigured.

May you be given wisdom for the eyes of your soul
To see this as a time of gracious harvesting.
May you have the passion to heal what has hurt you,
And allow it to come closer and become one with you.

May you have great dignity,
Sense how free you are;
Above all, may you be given the wonderful gift
Of meeting the eternal light that is within you.

May you be blessed;
And may you find a wonderful love
In your self for your self.

FOR DEATH

From the moment you were born,
Your death has walked beside you.
Though it seldom shows its face,
You still feel its empty touch
When fear invades your life,
Or what you love is lost
Or inner damage is incurred.

Yet when destiny draws you
Into these spaces of poverty,
And your heart stays generous
Until some door opens into the light,
You are quietly befriending your death;
So that you will have no need to fear
When your time comes to turn and leave.

That the silent presence of your death
Would call your life to attention,
Wake you up to how scarce your time is
And to the urgency to become free
And equal to the call of your destiny.

That you would gather yourself
And decide carefully
How you now can live
The life you would love
To look back on
From your deathbed.

To Learn from Animal Being

Nearer to the earth's heart,
Deeper within its silence:
Animals know this world
In a way we never will.

We who are ever
Distanced and distracted
By the parade of bright
Windows thought opens:
Their seamless presence
Is not fractured thus.

Stranded between time
Gone and time emerging,
We manage seldom
To be where we are:
Whereas they are always
Looking out from
The here and now.

May we learn to return
And rest in the beauty
Of animal being,
Learn to lean low,
Leave our locked minds,
And with freed senses
Feel the earth
Breathing with us.

May we enter
Into lightness of spirit,
And slip frequently into
The feel of the wild.

Let the clear silence
Of our animal being
Cleanse our hearts
Of corrosive words.

May we learn to walk
Upon the earth
With all their confidence
And clear-eyed stillness
So that our minds
Might be baptized
In the name of the wind
And the light and the rain.

IN PRAISE OF WATER

Let us bless the grace of water:

The imagination of the primeval ocean
Where the first forms of life stirred
And emerged to dress the vacant earth
With warm quilts of color.

The well whose liquid root worked
Through the long night of clay,
Trusting ahead of itself openings
That would yet yield to its yearning
Until at last it arises in the desire of light
To discover the pure quiver of itself
Flowing crystal clear and free
Through delighted emptiness.

The courage of a river to continue belief
In the slow fall of ground,
Always falling farther
Toward the unseen ocean.

The river does what words would love,
Keeping its appearance
By insisting on disappearance;
Its only life surrendered
To the event of pilgrimage,
Carrying the origin to the end,

Seldom pushing or straining,
Keeping itself to itself
Everywhere all along its flow,
All at one with its sinuous mind,
An utter rhythm, never awkward,
It continues to swirl
Through all unlikeness,
With elegance:
A ceaseless traverse of presence
Soothing on each side
The stilled fields,
Sounding out its journey,
Raising up a buried music
Where the silence of time
Becomes almost audible.

Tides stirred by the eros of the moon
Draw from that permanent restlessness
Perfect waves that languidly rise
And pleat in gradual forms of aquamarine
To offer every last tear of delight
At the altar of stillness inland.

And the rain in the night, driven
By the loneliness of the wind
To perforate the darkness,
As though some air pocket might open
To release the perfume of the lost day
And salvage some memory
From its forsaken turbulence

And drop its weight of longing
Into the earth, and anchor.

Let us bless the humility of water,
Always willing to take the shape
Of whatever otherness holds it,

The buoyancy of water
Stronger than the deadening,
Downward drag of gravity,
The innocence of water,
Flowing forth, without thought
Of what awaits it,
The refreshment of water,
Dissolving the crystals of thirst.

Water: voice of grief,
Cry of love,
In the flowing tear.

Water: vehicle and idiom
Of all the inner voyaging
That keeps us alive.

Blessed be water,
Our first mother.

4 • *Homecomings*

 There is an old shed near my house. Each April, after their long journey from Africa, the swallows return to the same nests in its rafters. They refurbish the nests and soon new little swallows will hatch out there. It is fascinating that the destination of such a huge continental journey is the fragile little grass-and-mud homes in the roof of an abandoned shed. It suggests that one can undertake any voyage if the destination is home. Humble or grand, home is where your heart belongs.

When it is a place of shelter and love, there is no place like home. It is then one of the sweetest words in any language. It suggests a nest where intimacy and belonging foster identity and individuality. In a sense, the notion of home is a continuation of the human body, which is, after all, our original and primary home on earth; it houses the mind, heart, and spirit. To be, we need to be home. When a place to belong is assured, the adventure of growth can begin with great promise.

Driving at dusk through the countryside, one sees the lights coming on in the different homes. One glimpses the bright interiors that house each family. The very ordinariness of these houses conceals the force and mystery of the events that unfold there. Very few other buildings house such transformation. A home is a subtle, implicit laboratory of spirit. It is here that human beings are made; here that their minds open to discover others and come to know who they might be themselves. It is astounding how the seminal happenings in life are mainly unconscious and implicit. Most of what happens within a home unfolds inside the ordinary narrative of the daily routine. Yet later on in life, when one looks back more closely, it is quite incredible how so many of the roots of one's identity, experience, and presence lead back to that childhood kitchen where so much was happening unknown to itself.

The origin of the word *dwell* is "to dig deep." Born into the home, the child starts from the deepest place. In the early silence of childhood, experience becomes deeply engraved. Whatever experience happens here modulates and sets the rhythm of mind and the sensitivities of the heart. If parents were aware of how much secretly depends on them, they would become paralyzed with the weight of responsibility. Home is where we start from, and it inevitably also determines how we start to be who we are. *The Oxford English Dictionary* states that home also means "a place where a thing flourishes or from which it originates." In such a subtle and unseen way the home is the seedbed of individual presence.

The simple act of walking into someone's home can be revelatory. You have stepped from the anonymity of the streets into the sudden, gathered intimacy of a private sanctuary. There is some unwarranted way in which the home displays the presences that it holds and molds. This visual is never available anywhere else. Outside the home its members become different in the various situations in which they find themselves. However, in the home the family as an intricate interweave of presences throws one another into unique relief. While this is usually subtle and can often be largely concealed, it can glimmer through in the immediacy of meeting them all together. If one could discern it, everything is there—on show. This is often the startling recognition looking back years later at family photographs. There one sees oneself as a child looking out at the camera from within your cluster of siblings, most likely innocent to all the psychological and spiritual forces that were at work.

There is nothing as un-neutral as a home. Even the most ordinary home is an implicit theater to subversive inner happenings. It is the most self-effacing laboratory of consciousness quietly shaping belief, expectation, and life direction. Parents are invisible creators. Quietly, day after day, their care and kindness nurture and foster the unseen landscapes of their children's minds. On the life journey of each individual the nature of the mind determines what is seen and valued. In *The Symposium*, Plato said so beautifully that one of the highest human privileges is to "be midwife to the birth of the soul in another." This is the precious and eternal work that parents do; they do this unobtrusively and continuously. Next to birth, bringing a child physically into the world, this is the greatest gift that one can confer on another. It is a gift that, once given, can never be taken away by anyone else, an inner gift that will inform and illuminate their journey.

There is no such thing as perfect parents. All parents

make mistakes and inevitably leave lesser or greater trails of damage. In later life it is often a painful and difficult task for a person to discern and integrate what occurred in childhood; this can be slow work, but it can yield great fruits of forgiveness, freedom, and tranquillity of heart.

Despite its huge inner significance for mind and soul, the home is also the locus of a poignant transience. In order to grow up, we have to learn to leave home. There is a beautiful short story by Liam O'Flaherty describing how a mother bird pushes her little ones out of the nest so that they might learn to fly. The wholeness of a home depends much on its ability to prepare its young to leave the nest and risk trusting their own wings to take them to unknown elsewheres, where they will have to build their individual nests. Eventually, parents encounter the challenge of dealing with the empty nest.

Home is where the heart is. It stands for the sure center where individual life is shaped and from where it journeys forth. What it ultimately intends is that each of its individuals would develop the capacity to be at home in themselves. This is something that is usually overlooked, but it is a vital requirement in the creativity and integrity of individual personality. It has to do with the essence of a person, their sense of their own inner ground. When a person is at home in his life, he always has a clear instinct about the shape of outer situations; even in the midst of confusion he can discern the traces of a path forward. When one is at home in oneself, one is integrated and enjoys a sense of balance and poise. In a sense that is exactly what spirituality is: the art of homecoming.

As a Child Enters the World

As I enter my new family,
May they be delighted
At how their kindness
Comes into blossom.

Unknown to me and them,
May I be exactly the one
To restore in their forlorn places
New vitality and promise.

May the hearts of others
Hear again the music
In the lost echoes
Of their neglected wonder.

If my destiny is sheltered,
May the grace of this privilege
Reach and bless the other infants
Who are destined for torn places.

If my destiny is bleak,
May I find in myself
A secret stillness
And tranquillity
Beneath the turmoil.

May my eyes never lose sight
Of why I have come here,

That I never be claimed
By the falsity of fear
Or eat the bread of bitterness.

In everything I do, think,
Feel, and say,
May I allow the light
Of the world I am leaving
To shine through and carry me home.

In Praise of the Earth

Let us bless
The imagination of the Earth.
That knew early the patience
To harness the mind of time,
Waited for the seas to warm,
Ready to welcome the emergence
Of things dreaming of voyaging
Among the stillness of land.

And how light knew to nurse
The growth until the face of the Earth
Brightened beneath a vision of color.

When the ages of ice came
And sealed the Earth inside
An endless coma of cold,
The heart of the Earth held hope,
Storing fragments of memory,
Ready for the return of the sun.

Let us thank the Earth
That offers ground for home
And holds our feet firm
To walk in space open
To infinite galaxies.

Let us salute the silence
And certainty of mountains:

Their sublime stillness,
Their dream-filled hearts.

The wonder of a garden
Trusting the first warmth of spring
Until its black infinity of cells
Becomes charged with dream;
Then the silent, slow nurture
Of the seed's self, coaxing it
To trust the act of death.

The humility of the Earth
That transfigures all
That has fallen
Of outlived growth.

The kindness of the Earth,
Opening to receive
Our worn forms
Into the final stillness.

Let us ask forgiveness of the Earth
For all our sins against her:
For our violence and poisonings
Of her beauty.

Let us remember within us
The ancient clay,
Holding the memory of seasons,
The passion of the wind,

The fluency of water,
The warmth of fire,
The quiver-touch of the sun
And shadowed sureness of the moon.

That we may awaken,
To live to the full
The dream of the Earth
Who chose us to emerge
And incarnate its hidden night
In mind, spirit, and light.

FOR A MOTHER

Mother,
Your voice learning to soothe
Your new child
Was the first home-sound
We heard before we could see.

Your young eyes
Gazing on us
Was the first mirror
Where we glimpsed
What to be seen
Could mean.

Mother,
Your nearness tilled the air,
An umbilical garden for all the seeds
Of thought that stirred in our infant hearts.

You nurtured and fostered this space
To root all our quietly gathering intensity
That could grow nowhere else.

Mother,
Formed from the depths beneath your heart,
You know us from the inside out.
No deeds or seas or others
Could ever erase that.

FOR A FATHER

The longer we live,
The more of your presence
We find, laid down,
Weave upon weave
Within our lives.

The quiet constancy of your gentleness
Drew no attention to itself,
Yet filled our home
With a climate of kindness
Where each mind felt free
To seek its own direction.

As the fields of distance
Opened inside childhood,
Your presence was a sheltering tree
Where our fledgling hearts could rest.

The earth seemed to trust your hands
As they tilled the soil, put in the seed,
Gathered together the lonely stones.

Something in you loved to inquire
In the neighborhood of air,
Searching its transparent rooms
For the fallen glances of God.

The warmth and wonder of your prayer
Opened our eyes to glimpse
The subtle ones who
Are eternally there.

Whenever, silently, in off moments,
The beauty of the whole thing overcame you,
You would gaze quietly out upon us,
The look from your eyes
Like a kiss alighting on skin.

There are many things
We could have said,
But words never wanted
To name them;
And perhaps a world
That is quietly sensed
Across the air
In another's heart
Becomes the inner companion
To one's own unknown.

GRACE BEFORE MEALS

As we begin this meal with grace,
Let us become aware of the memory
Carried inside the food before us:
The quiver of the seed
Awakening in the earth,
Unfolding in a trust of roots
And slender stems of growth,
On its voyage toward harvest,
The kiss of rain and surge of sun;
The innocence of animal soul
That never spoke a word,
Nourished by the earth
To become today our food;
The work of all the strangers
Whose hands prepared it,
The privilege of wealth and health
That enables us to feast and celebrate.

GRACE AFTER MEALS

We end this meal with grace
For the joy and nourishment of food,
The slowed time away from the world
To come into presence with each other
And sense the subtle lives behind our faces,
The different colors of our voices,
The edges of hungers we keep private,
The circle of love that unites us.
We pray the wise spirit who keeps us
To change the structures that make others hunger
And that after such grace we might now go forth
And impart dignity wherever we partake.

FOR A BROTHER OR A SISTER

The knowing that binds us
Is older than the apostrophe of cell
We formed from within the one womb.

All that flowed into us there
From the red village of ancestry
Sowed spores of continuity
That would one day flower
Into flickers of resemblance:

An unconscious gesture
Could echo an ancestor,
And the look of us stir
Recognition of belonging
That is ours alone;

And our difference finding
Its own rhythm of strangeness,
Leading us deeper into a self
That would always know its own
Regardless of difficulty and distance;
And through hurt no other could inflict;

Still somehow beside each other
Though the night is dark
With wind that loves
To clean the bones of ruins,
Making further room for light.

ON WAKING

I give thanks for arriving
Safely in a new dawn,
For the gift of eyes
To see the world,
The gift of mind
To feel at home
In my life.
The waves of possibility
Breaking on the shore of dawn,
The harvest of the past
That awaits my hunger,
And all the furtherings
This new day will bring.

On Meeting a Stranger

With respect
And reverence
That the unknown
Between us
Might flower
Into discovery
And lead us
Beyond
The familiar field
Blind with the weed
Of weariness
And the old walls
Of habit.

On Passing a Graveyard

May perpetual light shine upon
The faces of all who rest here.

May the lives they lived
Unfold further in spirit.

May all their past travails
Find ease in the kindness of clay.

May the remembering earth
Mind every memory they brought.

May the rains from the heavens
Fall gently upon them.

May the wildflowers and grasses
Whisper their wishes into light.

May we reverence the village of presence
In the stillness of this silent field.

To Come Home to Yourself

May all that is unforgiven in you
Be released.

May your fears yield
Their deepest tranquillities.

May all that is unlived in you
Blossom into a future
Graced with love.

At the End of the Day:
A Mirror of Questions

What dreams did I create last night?
Where did my eyes linger today?
Where was I blind?
Where was I hurt without anyone noticing?
What did I learn today?
What did I read?
What new thoughts visited me?
What differences did I notice in those closest to me?
Whom did I neglect?
Where did I neglect myself?
What did I begin today that might endure?
How were my conversations?
What did I do today for the poor and the excluded?
Did I remember the dead today?
Where could I have exposed myself to the risk of
    something different?
Where did I allow myself to receive love?
With whom today did I feel most myself?
What reached me today? How deep did it imprint?
Who saw me today?
What visitations had I from the past and from the
    future?
What did I avoid today?
From the evidence—why was I given this day?

Before Sleep

As I lay down to sleep,
May the guardian angel
Watch over me,
Coaxing all my cares
To unravel into peace.

As darkness within
Is wed to darkness without,
Freed from the weight of light,
Let my eyes sleep,
Relieved of all intensities.

Let my imagination
Trawl the compressed seas
To bless the dawn
With a generous catch
Of luminous dream.

May this new night of rest
Repair the wear of time
And restore youth of heart
For the adventure
That awaits tomorrow.

5 • *States of Heart*

The human body is an amazing masterpiece. With the senses we see, taste, and touch the world, drawing its mystery inside us. With the mind we probe the eternal structures of things. With the face we present ourselves to the world and recognize one another. But it is the heart that makes us human.

The heart is where the beauty of the human spirit comes alive. Without the heart, the human would be sinister. To be able to feel is the great gift. When you feel for someone, you become united with that person in an intimate way; your concern and compassion come alive, drawing some of the other person's world and spirit into yours. Feeling is the secret bridge that penetrates solitude and isolation. Without the ability to feel, friendship and love could never be born. All feeling is born in the heart. This makes the human heart the true jewel of the world.

Facing outward, the senses are in ever new conversation with whatever surrounds us. Facing possibility, the mind is in relentless thought-flow. Concealed within the dark, the heart is concerned with who we are. It is ever attentive to how we feel; it senses and feels where the care, the joy, the fear, and the tenderness reside. Always and at every point, the heart remembers who we are. Though so much else is in motion in the mind and the senses, the hidden heart never loses sight of us. If we ever feel lost or overwhelmed, all we have to do is become still and listen in to our heart and we will soon find exactly where we are.

Because the mind is always engaged with whatever is happening now, it often forgets who we are. The heart never forgets. Everything of significance is inscribed there. The heart is the archive of all our intimate memory. What is truly felt leaves the deepest inscription. Each of us carries the book of our life inside our heart. Often at night when we dream, we are surprised at how clearly versions of long-forgotten events return with strange clarity. Though we live much of our lives outside, in action and engagement with the world, the deeper impact of what happens is registered in the narrative of the heart.

Because the heart dwells in unattended dark, we often forget its sublime sensitivity to everything that is happening to us. Without our ever noticing, the heart absorbs the joy of things and also their pain and care. Within us, therefore, a burdening can accrue. For this reason it is wise now and again to tune in to your heart and listen for what it carries. Sometimes the simplest things effect unexpected transformation. The old people here used to say that a burden shared is a burden halved. Similarly, when you allow your heart to speak, the burdens it carries diminish, a new lightness enters your body, and relief floods the heart. In his poem "In Memory of W. B. Yeats," W. H. Auden has the beautiful quatrain:

In the deserts of the heart
Let the healing fountain start,
In the prison of his days
Teach the free man how to praise.

It brings great joy to feel alive. You sense the beauty and privilege of being here. For a while your eyes take in the world in all its adventure and grace; you feel somehow at the center of its surge of invitation and possibility. One of the loneliest elements of exile is the exile from one's feelings. The person who is not able to feel his life has become dangerously dislocated. Sometimes severe suffering causes this numbing; the heart atrophies.

The shape of the human heart is very distinctive; it is an instantly recognizable image. It is an interesting shape. Neither a circle nor a triangle, it somehow manages to blend both contours. Viewed through the metaphor of the triangle, the heart is a space where the self and its otherness unite to configure the individual presence of the person. This threefold structure is also the structure at work in friendship and love: you, the friend, and the triangle is completed in the "third force," which is the spirit of the friendship; this is more than the sum of the two dimensions. It is a force that has its own independence and a different tone of spirit. Therefore, outer and inner friendship have a triadic structure. In Christian belief, God is not a lonely divine object; rather God is where self and other, the one and the many, come together. God is three persons in a kinetic flow of originating, enduring, and completing love.

The Father generates the Son, and both together create the Spirit, who is the third force where their knowing, narrative, and memory unite. The first heart is the Sacred Heart.

Viewed through the metaphor of the circle, other qualities of the heart come into relief. The heart has a beautiful simultaneity, being at once the place of arrival and departure within the body. All the wearied blood arrives there to be refreshed and renewed, and it is from this place that the newly invigorated life force sets forth. It is the place of ending that is always a new beginning. The circle is an ancient form; it signifies continuity, belonging, and permanence. It is consoling to think that at the center of the human body the heart holds one's life within its sure circle.

The state of one's heart inevitably shapes one's life; it is ultimately the place where everything is decided.

- A courageous heart will go forth and engage with life despite confusion and fear.
- A fearful heart will be hesitant and will tend to hold back.
- A heavy heart will make for a gloomy, unlived life.
- A compassionate heart need never carry the burden of judgment.
- A forgiving heart knows the art of liberation.
- A loving heart awakens the spirit of possibility and engagement with others.

The power of the heart's attitude is expressed beautifully in the New Testament: "Where your treasure is, there is your heart also." And all through the Old Testament, God is interested only in the heart—not sacrifices, rituals, or rules—only the heart. Indeed, the mystical tradition would suggest the heart is beautiful precisely because it is where God dwells: the heart is the divine sanctuary.

FOR COURAGE

When the light around you lessens
And your thoughts darken until
Your body feels fear turn
Cold as a stone inside,

When you find yourself bereft
Of any belief in yourself
And all you unknowingly
Leaned on has fallen,

When one voice commands
Your whole heart,
And it is raven dark,

Steady yourself and see
That it is your own thinking
That darkens your world,

Search and you will find
A diamond-thought of light,

Know that you are not alone
And that this darkness has purpose;
Gradually it will school your eyes
To find the one gift your life requires
Hidden within this night-corner.

Invoke the learning
Of every suffering
You have suffered.

Close your eyes.
Gather all the kindling
About your heart
To create one spark.
That is all you need
To nourish the flame
That will cleanse the dark
Of its weight of festered fear.

A new confidence will come alive
To urge you toward higher ground
Where your imagination
Will learn to engage difficulty
As its most rewarding threshold!

FOR AN EXILE

When you dream, it is always home.
You are there among your own,
The rhythm of their voices rising like song
Your blood would sing through any dark.

Then you awake to find yourself listening
To the sounds of traffic in another land.
For a moment your whole body recoils
At the strange emptiness of where you are.

This country is cold to your voice.
It is still a place without echoes.
Nothing of yours has happened here.

No one knows you,
The language slows you,
The thick accent smothers your presence.

You sound foreign to yourself;
Their eyes reflect how strange you seem
When seen across a cold distance
That has no bridge to carry
The charisma in which your friends
Delight at home.

Though your work here is hard,
It brings relief, helps your mind
In returning to the small
Bounties of your absence.

Evening is without protection;
Your room waits,
Ready to take you
Back like some convict
Who is afraid
Of the life outside.

The things you brought from home
Look back at you; out of place here
They take on lonely power.

You cringe at the thought
That someone from home
Might see you now here,
In this unsheltered room.

Now is the time to hold faithful
To your dream, to understand
That this is an interim time
Full of awkward disconnection.

Gradually you will come to find
Your way to friends who will open
Doors into a new belonging.

Your heart will brighten
With new discovery,
Your presence will unclench
And find ease,
Letting your substance
And promise be seen.

Slowly, a new world will open for you.
The eyes of your heart, refined
By this desert time, will be free
To see and celebrate the new life
For which you sacrificed everything.

For Solitude

May you recognize in your life the presence,
power, and light of your soul.

May you realize that you are never alone,
that your soul in its brightness and belonging
connects you intimately with the rhythm of the
     universe.

May you have respect for your individuality and
     difference.

May you realize that the shape of your soul is
     unique,
that you have a special destiny here,
that behind the facade of your life
there is something beautiful and eternal happening.

May you learn to see your self
with the same delight,
pride, and expectation
with which God sees you in every moment.

For an Addict

On its way through the innocent night,
The moth is ambushed by the light,
Becomes glued to a window
Where a candle burns; its whole self,
Its dreams of flight and all desire
Trapped in one glazed gaze;
Now nothing else can satisfy
But the deadly beauty of flame.

When you lose the feel
For all other belonging
And what is truly near
Becomes distant and ghostly,
And you are visited
And claimed by a simplicity
Sinister in its singularity,

No longer yourself, your mind
And will owned and steered
From elsewhere now,
You would sacrifice anything
To dance once more to the haunted
Music with your fatal beloved
Who owns the eyes of your heart.

These words of blessing cannot
Reach, even as echoes,
To the shore of where you are,

Yet may they work without you
To soften some slight line through
To the white cave where
Your soul is captive.

May some glimmer
Of outside light reach your eyes
To help you recognize how
You have fallen for a vampire.

May you crash hard and soon
Onto real ground again
Where this fundamentalist
Shell might start to crack
For you to hear
Again your own echo.

That your lost lonesome heart
Might learn to cry out
For the true intimacy
Of love that waits
To take you home

To where you are known
And seen and where
Your life is treasured
Beyond every frontier
Of despair you have crossed.

For Failure

The will of color loves how light spreads
Through its diffusions, making textures subtle,
Clothing a landscape in concealment
For color to keep its mysteries
Hidden from the unready eye.

But the light that comes after rain
Is always fierce and clear,
And illuminates the face of everything
Through the transparency of rain.

Despite the initial darkening,
This is the light that failure casts.
Beholden no more to the promise
Of what dream and work would bring.
It shows where roots have withered
And where the source has gone dry.
The light of failure has no mercy
On the affections of the heart;
It emerges from beyond the personal,
A wiry, forthright light that likes to see crevices
Open in the shell of a controlled life.

Though cruel now, it serves a deeper kindness,
Wise to the larger call of growth.

It invites us to humility
And the painstaking work of acceptance

So that one day we may look back
In recognition and appreciation
At the disappointment we now endure.

FOR GRIEF

When you lose someone you love,
Your life becomes strange,
The ground beneath you gets fragile,
Your thoughts make your eyes unsure;
And some dead echo drags your voice down
Where words have no confidence.

Your heart has grown heavy with loss;
And though this loss has wounded others too,
No one knows what has been taken from you
When the silence of absence deepens.

Flickers of guilt kindle regret
For all that was left unsaid or undone.

There are days when you wake up happy;
Again inside the fullness of life,
Until the moment breaks
And you are thrown back
Onto the black tide of loss.

Days when you have your heart back,
You are able to function well
Until in the middle of work or encounter,
Suddenly with no warning,
You are ambushed by grief.

It becomes hard to trust yourself.
All you can depend on now is that

Sorrow will remain faithful to itself.
More than you, it knows its way
And will find the right time
To pull and pull the rope of grief
Until that coiled hill of tears
Has reduced to its last drop.

Gradually, you will learn acquaintance
With the invisible form of your departed;
And when the work of grief is done,
The wound of loss will heal
And you will have learned
To wean your eyes
From that gap in the air
And be able to enter the hearth
In your soul where your loved one
Has awaited your return
All the time.

FOR THE INTERIM TIME

When near the end of day, life has drained
Out of light, and it is too soon
For the mind of night to have darkened things,

No place looks like itself, loss of outline
Makes everything look strangely in-between,
Unsure of what has been, or what might come.

In this wan light, even trees seem groundless.
In a while it will be night, but nothing
Here seems TO believe the relief of dark.

You are in this time of the interim
Where everything seems withheld.

The path you took to get here has washed out;
The way forward is still concealed from you.

"The old is not old enough to have died away;
The new is still too young to be born."

You cannot lay claim to anything;
In this place of dusk,
Your eyes are blurred;
And there is no mirror.

Everyone else has lost sight of your heart
And you can see nowhere to put your trust;
You know you have to make your own way through.

As far as you can, hold your confidence.
Do not allow your confusion to squander
This call which is loosening
Your roots in false ground,
That you might come free
From all you have outgrown.

What is being transfigured here is your mind,
And it is difficult and slow to become new.
The more faithfully you can endure here,
The more refined your heart will become
For your arrival in the new dawn.

FOR BEAUTY

As stillness in stone to silence is wed,
May solitude foster your truth in word.

As a river flows in ideal sequence,
May your soul reveal where time is presence.

As the moon absolves the dark of distance,
May your style of thought bridge the difference.

As the breath of light awakens color,
May the dawn anoint your eyes with wonder.

As spring rain softens the earth with surprise,
May your winter places be kissed by light.

As the ocean dreams to the joy of dance,
May the grace of change bring you elegance.

As clay anchors a tree in light and wind,
May your outer life grow from peace within.

As twilight pervades the belief of night,
May beauty sleep lightly within your heart.

Caged in a cold, functional cell,
Far from the comfort of home
With none of your own things,
In a place that is gray and grim,
Where sounds are seldom gentle,
Amidst the shuffle of dumbed feet,
The crossword of lost voices,
The one constant note
Is the dead, trap-shut sound
Of unrelenting doors that
Make walls absolute.

Though you have lost the outside world,
May you discover the untold journey
That awaits you in the inner world.

May you come to recognize
That though your body is imprisoned,
No one can imprison your mind.

May all the time you have on your hands
Bring you into new friendship with your mind
So that you learn to understand and integrate
The darkness that brought you here.

Within this limited space,
May you learn to harness
The stretch of time.

May your compassion awaken.
May you learn to recover the self
You were before you lost your way
And draw from its depths
Some balm to heal your wounds.

Behind the harsh rhythms of prison life,
May you find a friend you can talk to
And nurture the natural kindness
To become more free in your heart
And lighten the outer constraints.

May your eyes look up and find
The bright line of an inner horizon
That will ground and encourage you
For that distant day when your new feet
Will step out onto the pastures of freedom.

For Suffering

May you be blessed in the holy names of those
Who, without you knowing it,
Help to carry and lighten your pain.

May you know serenity
When you are called
To enter the house of suffering.

May a window of light always surprise you.

May you be granted the wisdom
To avoid false resistance;
When suffering knocks on the door of your life,
May you glimpse its eventual gifts.

May you be able to receive the fruits of suffering.

May memory bless and protect you
With the hard-earned light of past travail;
To remind you that you have survived before
And though the darkness now is deep,
You will soon see approaching light.

May the grace of time heal your wounds.

May you know that though the storm might rage,
Not a hair of your head will be harmed.

For One Who Is Exhausted

When the rhythm of the heart becomes hectic,
Time takes on the strain until it breaks;
Then all the unattended stress falls in
On the mind like an endless, increasing weight.

The light in the mind becomes dim.
Things you could take in your stride before
Now become laborsome events of will.

Weariness invades your spirit.
Gravity begins falling inside you,
Dragging down every bone.

The tide you never valued has gone out.
And you are marooned on unsure ground.
Something within you has closed down;
And you cannot push yourself back to life.

You have been forced to enter empty time.
The desire that drove you has relinquished.
There is nothing else to do now but rest
And patiently learn to receive the self
You have forsaken in the race of days.

At first your thinking will darken
And sadness take over like listless weather.
The flow of unwept tears will frighten you.

You have traveled too fast over false ground;
Now your soul has come to take you back.

Take refuge in your senses, open up
To all the small miracles you rushed through.

Become inclined to watch the way of rain
When it falls slow and free.

Imitate the habit of twilight,
Taking time to open the well of color
That fostered the brightness of day.

Draw alongside the silence of stone
Until its calmness can claim you.
Be excessively gentle with yourself.

Stay clear of those vexed in spirit.
Learn to linger around someone of ease
Who feels they have all the time in the world.

Gradually, you will return to yourself,
Having learned a new respect for your heart
And the joy that dwells far within slow time.

FOR EQUILIBRIUM

Like the joy of the sea coming home to shore,
May the relief of laughter rinse through your soul.

As the wind loves to call things to dance,
May your gravity be lightened by grace.

Like the dignity of moonlight restoring the earth,
May your thoughts incline with reverence and respect.

As water takes whatever shape it is in,
So free may you be about who you become.

As silence smiles on the other side of what's said,
May your sense of irony bring perspective.

As time remains free of all that it frames,
May your mind stay clear of all it names.

May your prayer of listening deepen enough
To hear in the depths the laughter of God.

For Loneliness

When the light lessens,
Causing colors to lose their courage,
And your eyes fix on the empty distance
That can open on either side
Of the surest line
To make all that is
Familiar and near
Seem suddenly foreign,

When the music of talk
Breaks apart into noise
And you hear your heart louden
While the voices around you
Slow down to leaden echoes
Turning the silence
Into something stony and cold,

When the old ghosts come back
To feed on everywhere you felt sure,
Do not strengthen their hunger
By choosing to fear;
Rather, decide to call on your heart
That it may grow clear and free
To welcome home your emptiness
That it may cleanse you
Like the clearest air
You could ever breathe.

Allow your loneliness time
To dissolve the shell of dross
That had closed around you;
Choose in this severe silence
To hear the one true voice
Your rushed life fears;
Cradle yourself like a child
Learning to trust what emerges,
So that gradually
You may come to know
That deep in that black hole
You will find the blue flower
That holds the mystical light
Which will illuminate in you
The glimmer of springtime.

6 • Callings

Someone asked me recently: What is it that haunts you? I said, "I can tell you exactly; it is the sense of time slipping through my fingers like fine sand. And there is nothing I can do to slow it." One of the Psalms prays: "O Lord, help me to see the shortness of life that I may gain wisdom of heart." As we get older, time seems to speed up. The sense of transience haunts nearly every heart. You feel that you could suddenly arrive at your last day incredulous that that was it; it was all over.

From time immemorial it has been one of the deepest longings of the human heart to strain against the erosion of one's life, to find a way of living and being that manages to find some stable ground within time, a place from where something eternal can be harvested from our disappearance. This is what all art strives for: the creation of a living permanence. It is what we are secretly doing when we become parents: endeavoring to maintain our continuity beyond our own ending. The harvesting of transience is what we also are attempting in choosing the form of life we live. When we arrive on earth, we are provided with no map for our life journey. Only gradually, as our identity forms and we get an inkling of who we are, do possibilities begin to emerge that call us. It is one of the weightiest decisions: to decide what to do with your life. The challenge is to find a way of life that will be in harmony with your gifts and needs.

Behind each face there is a unique world that no one else can see. This is the mystery of individuality. The shape of each soul is different. No one else feels your life the way you do. No one else sees or hears the world as you do. The creation of the individual is a divine masterpiece. We were dreamed for a long time before we were born. Our souls, minds, and hearts fashioned in the divine imagination. Such care and attention went into the creation of each person. Given the uniqueness of each of us, it should not be surprising that one of the greatest challenges is to inhabit our own individuality and to discover which life-form best expresses it.

The great law of life is: Be yourself. Though this axiom sounds simple, it is often a difficult task. To be yourself, you have to learn how to become who you were dreamed to be. Each person has a unique destiny. To be born is to be chosen. There is something special that each of us has to do in the world. If someone else could do it, they would be here and not us. One of the fascinating questions is to decipher what one's destiny is. At the heart of each destiny is hidden a unique life calling. What is it you are called to do? In old-fashioned language: What is your vocation in life?

For some people, the question of their calling is very difficult to decipher; for others, it follows from an early intuition and practically unfolds of its own accord. For some, it can be the singular and exclusive direction their life takes; for others, it can change and follow new directions.

Again, some people never seem to find what they are called to do; this can burden them with a continual restlessness and dissatisfaction. When you find what you are called to do, your life takes on a focus and purpose. You come into rhythm with the deeper longing of your heart.

The notion of vocation is interesting and rich. It suggests that there is a special form of life that one is called to; to follow this is the way to realize one's destiny. Following one's vocation ensures that what you choose to do finds itself in harmony with your inner nature. It also means that this is the optimum way to unfold and develop whatever gifts one has. A vocation does not clear before you a smooth path through difficulties. Having a sense of one's vocation does not in any way relieve one of the travail and turbulence of being human. Indeed, being true to one's vocation can often require a level of generosity and risk that will cause great suffering, for more often than not there is no surge of light to clarify direction; the light on offer is enough to guide only the next step.

The nature of the calling can change over time, taking a person down pathways never anticipated. The calling opens new territories within the heart; this in turn deepens the calling itself. The faces of the calling change; what at the beginning seemed simple and clear can become ambivalent and complex as it unfolds. To develop a heart that is generous and equal to this complexity is the continual challenge of growth. This is the creative tension that dwells at the heart of vocation. One is urged and coaxed beyond the pale regions into rich territories of risk and promise.

It is devastating to feel trapped in a form of life where

you feel utterly misplaced and all your effort is labored; everything you do is done against the grain. You take no joy or pleasure in what you do, and your heart is haunted by alternative lives you will never have. When you feel like this it can make for a resentful and bitter life—a life where you are neither seen nor understood for much of the time—and your gifts remain locked away, never to emerge. It is clearly time to change what you are doing, perhaps sacrifice the familiar in order to find your true calling. Such change can utterly transform your life. It is such a relief and joy to find the calling that expresses and incarnates your spirit. When you find that you are doing what you love, what you were brought here to do, it makes for a rich and contented life. You have come into rhythm with your longing. Your work and action emerge naturally; you don't have to force yourself. Your energy is immediate. Your passion is clear and creative. A new calling can open the door into the house of vision and belonging. You feel at home in your life, heart and hearth at one.

FOR PRIESTHOOD

May the blessings released through your hands
Cause windows to open in darkened minds.

May the sufferings your calling brings
Be but winter before the spring.

May the companionship of your doubt
Restore what your beliefs leave out.

May the secret hungers of your heart
Harvest from emptiness its sacred fruit.

May your solitude be a voyage
Into the wilderness and wonder of God.

May your words have the prophetic edge
To enable the heart to hear itself.

May the silence where your calling dwells
Foster your freedom in all you do and feel.

May you find words full of divine warmth
To clothe the dying in the language of dawn.

May the slow light of the Eucharist
Be a sure shelter around your future.

As spring unfolds the dream of the earth,
May you bring each other's hearts to birth.

As the ocean finds calm in view of land,
May you love the gaze of each other's mind.

As the wind arises free and wild,
May nothing negative control your lives.

As kindly as moonlight might search the dark,
So gentle may you be when light grows scarce.

As surprised as the silence that music opens,
May your words for each other be touched with
     reverence.

As warmly as the air draws in the light,
May you welcome each other's every gift.

As elegant as dream absorbing the night,
May sleep find you clear of anger and hurt.

As twilight harvests all the day's color,
May love bring you home to each other.

Elemental Blessing for a New Home

Before a human voice was ever heard here,
This place has known the respect of stone,
The friendship of the wind, always returning
With news of elsewhere, whispered in seed and
     pollen,
The thin symphonies of birdsong softening the
     silence,
The litanies of rain rearranging the air,
Cascades of sunlight opening and closing days,
And the glow of the moon gazing through
     darkness.
May all that elemental enrichment
Bless the foundation and standing of your home.

Before you came here, this place has known
The wonder of children's eyes,
The hope of mornings in troubled hearts,
The tranquillity of twilight easing the night,
The drama of dreams under sleeping eyelids,
The generous disturbance of birth,
The anxieties of old age unclenching into grace
And the final elegance of calmly embraced death.
May the life of your new home enter
Into this inheritance of spirit.

May the rain fall kindly,
May daylight illuminate your hearts,
May the darkness never burden,

May those who dwell here in the unseen
Watch over your coming and going,
May your lives of love and promise
Refine and deepen the mind of this land.

For the Farmer

Before the human mind could warm to itself,
The hands of the farmer had first to work,
Creating clearances in the earth's thicket:
Cut into the thorn-screens of wild briar,
Uproot the clusters of scrub-bush,
Dig out loose rock until a field emerged
Whose clay could be loosened and softened
To take seed and bring forth crops.

The earth was able to trust
The intention of the farmer's hands,
Opening it, softening it, molding it
Into a domain of shelter and nourishment.
It waits through its secluded winter
For his imagination of springtime
To feed into its darkened heart
New seeds for it to work its mind on
Until the harvest gathers and thickens
With golden corn, honey-scented hay,
Ripe red and dark purple fruit.

In his mind, his fields become presences;
The feel of their colors, the brace of their walls
Have greened his thought and tempered his heart.

His eyes can read the animal atmosphere;
And see through their silence to sense their minds.
His skilled hands can guide calves and lambs to
    birth.

Out among his animals, in rain, cold, and snow,
Talking to them in affectionate callings,
Something in him tuned to their rhythm.

In these times when geography becomes virtual
And developers urbanize the earth,
May the farmer continue to hold true ground,
Keeping the intimate knowing of the clay alive,
Nourishing us with the fruits of the earth,
Serving as custodian of that precious threshold
     where
The rhythm of nature with its serene pulse
And sublime patience restores our minds.

FOR A NURSE

Your mind knows the world of illness,
The fright that invades a person
Arriving in out of the world,
Distraught and grieved by illness.
How it can strip a life of its joy,
Dim the light of the heart
Put shock in the eyes.

You see worlds breaking
At the onset of illness:

Families at bedsides distraught
That their mother's name has come up
In the secret lottery of misfortune
That had always chosen someone else.
You watch their helpless love
That would exchange places with her.

The veil of skin opened,
The search through the body's night
To remove tissue, war-torn with cancer.

Young lives that should be out in the sun
Enjoying life with wild hearts,
Come in here lamed by accident
And the lucky ones who leave,
Already old and in captive posture.

The elderly, who should be prepared,
But are frightened and unsure.
You understand no one
Can learn beforehand
An elegant or easy way to die.

In this fragile frontier-place, your kindness
Becomes a light that consoles the brokenhearted,
Awakens within desperate storms
That oasis of serenity that calls
The spirit to rise from beneath the weight of pain,
To create a new space in the person's mind
Where they gain distance from their suffering
And begin to see the invitation
To integrate and transform it.

May you embrace the beauty in what you do
And how you stand like a secret angel
Between the bleak despair of illness
And the unquenchable light of spirit
That can turn the darkest destiny towards dawn.

May you never doubt the gifts you bring;
Rather, learn from these frontiers
Wisdom for your own heart.
May you come to inherit
The blessings of your kindness
And never be without care and love
When winter enters your own life.

For the Time of Necessary Decision

The mind of time is hard to read.
We can never predict what it will bring,
Nor even from all that is already gone
Can we say what form it finally takes;
For time gathers its moments secretly.
Often we only know it's time to change
When a force has built inside the heart
That leaves us uneasy as we are.

Perhaps the work we do has lost its soul
Or the love where we once belonged
Calls nothing alive in us anymore.

We drift through this gray, increasing nowhere
Until we stand before a threshold we know
We have to cross to come alive once more.

May we have the courage to take the step
Into the unknown that beckons us;
Trust that a richer life awaits us there,
That we will lose nothing
But what has already died;
Feel the deeper knowing in us sure
Of all that is about to be born beyond
The pale frames where we stayed confined,
Not realizing how such vacant endurance
Was bleaching our soul's desire.

For the Unknown Self

So much of what delights and troubles you
Happens on a surface
You take for ground.
Your mind thinks your life alone,
Your eyes consider air your nearest neighbor,
Yet it seems that a little below your heart
There houses in you an unknown self
Who prefers the patterns of the dark
And is not persuaded by the eye's affection
Or caught by the flash of thought.

It is a self that enjoys contemplative patience
With all your unfolding expression,
Is never drawn to break into light
Though you entangle yourself in unworthiness
And misjudge what you do and who you are.

It presides within like an evening freedom
That will often see you enchanted by twilight
Without ever recognizing the falling night,
It resembles the under-earth of your visible life:
All you do and say and think is fostered
Deep in its opaque and prevenient clay.

It dwells in a strange, yet rhythmic ease
That is not ruffled by disappointment;
It presides in a deeper current of time
Free from the force of cause and sequence
That otherwise shapes your life.

Were it to break forth into day,
Its dark light might quench your mind,
For it knows how your primeval heart
Sisters every cell of your life
To all your known mind would avoid,

Thus it knows to dwell in you gently,
Offering you only discrete glimpses
Of how you construct your life.

At times, it will lead you strangely,
Magnetized by some resonance
That ambushes your vigilance.

It works most resolutely at night
As the poet who draws your dreams,
Creating for you many secret doors,
Decorated with pictures of your hunger;

It has the dignity of the angelic
That knows you to your roots,
Always awaiting your deeper befriending
To take you beyond the threshold of want,
Where all your diverse strainings
Can come to wholesome ease.

FOR WORK

May the light of your soul bless your work
with love and warmth of heart.

May you see in what you do the beauty of your soul.

May the sacredness of your work bring light and
     renewal
to those who work with you
and to those who see and receive your work.

May your work never exhaust you.

May it release wellsprings of refreshment,
inspiration, and excitement.

May you never become lost in bland absences.

May the day never burden.

May dawn find hope in your heart,
approaching your new day with dreams,
possibilities, and promises.

May evening find you gracious and fulfilled.

May you go into the night blessed,
sheltered, and protected.

May your soul calm, console, and renew you.

May the gift of leadership awaken in you as a
    vocation,
Keep you mindful of the providence that calls you to
    serve.

As high over the mountains the eagle spreads its
    wings,
May your perspective be larger than the view from
    the foothills.

When the way is flat and dull in times of gray
    endurance,
May your imagination continue to evoke horizons.

When thirst burns in times of drought,
May you be blessed to find the wells.

May you have the wisdom to read time clearly
And know when the seed of change will flourish.

In your heart may there be a sanctuary
For the stillness where clarity is born.

May your work be infused with passion and creativity
And have the wisdom to balance compassion and
    challenge.

May your soul find the graciousness
To rise above the fester of small mediocrities.
May your power never become a shell
Wherein your heart would silently atrophy.
May you welcome your own vulnerability
As the ground where healing and truth join.

May integrity of soul be your first ideal,
The source that will guide and bless your work.

In these times when anger
Is turned into anxiety
And someone has stolen
The horizons and mountains,

Our small emperors on parade
Never expect our indifference
To disturb their nakedness.

They keep their heads down
And their eyes gleam with reflection
From aluminum economic ground,

The media wraps everything
In a cellophane of sound,
And the ghost surface of the virtual
Overlays the breathing earth.

The industry of distraction
Makes us forget
That we live in a universe.

We have become converts
To the religion of stress
And its deity of progress;

That we may have courage
To turn aside from it all

And come to kneel down before the poor,
To discover what we must do,
How to turn anxiety
Back into anger,
How to find our way home.

May you have the grace and wisdom
To act kindly, learning
To distinguish between what is
Personal and what is not.

May you be hospitable to criticism.

May you never put yourself at the center of things.

May you act not from arrogance but out of service.

May you work on yourself,
Building up and refining the ways of your mind.

May those who work for you know
You see and respect them.

May you learn to cultivate the art of presence
In order to engage with those who meet you.

When someone fails or disappoints you,
May the graciousness with which you engage
Be their stairway to renewal and refinement.

May you treasure the gifts of the mind
Through reading and creative thinking
So that you continue as a servant of the frontier

Where the new will draw its enrichment from the
    old,
And you never become a functionary.

May you know the wisdom of deep listening,
The healing of wholesome words,
The encouragement of the appreciative gaze,
The decorum of held dignity,
The springtime edge of the bleak question.

May you have a mind that loves frontiers
So that you can evoke the bright fields
That lie beyond the view of the regular eye.

May you have good friends
To mirror your blind spots.

May leadership be for you
A true adventure of growth.

Alive to the thrill
Of the wild.

Meet the dawn
On a mountain.

Wash your face
In the morning dew.

Feel the favor of the earth.

Go out naked in the wind,
Your skin
Almost Aeolian.

With the music inside,
Dance like there is no outside.

Become subtle enough
To hear a tree breathe.

Sleep by the ocean,
Letting yourself unfurl
Like the reeds that swirl
Gradually on the sea floor.

Try to watch a painting from within:
How it holds what it never shows.

The mystery of your face,
Showing what you never see.

See your imagination dawn
Around the rim of your world.

Feel the seamless silk of the ocean
Womb you in ancient buoyancy.

Feel the wild imprint of surprise
When you are taken in by your lover's eyes.

Succumb to warmth in the heart
Where divine fire glows.

7 · Beyond Endings

Endings seem to lie in wait. Absorbed in our experience, we forget that an ending might be approaching. Consequently, when the ending signals its arrival, we can feel ambushed. Perhaps there is an instinctive survival mechanism in us that distracts us from the inevitability of ending, thus enabling us to live in the present with an innocence and wholeheartedness. Were we to be haunted by the prospect of ending, we could not give ourselves with freedom and passion.

Endings are strange. Usually they leave us disturbed and bereft. For instance, when we look back on a relationship that ended, there is often such a contrast between the innocence and joy of how it initially unfolded and the soreness and protrusion of its ending. Back then we could never have imagined or foreseen such an ending. Yet somehow within it the seed of such a conclusion must have been already germinating. How quietly and irreversibly inevitability can build within something; during each new stage it is strengthening its grip on finality. Sometimes in the unfolding of a situation, there can be a moment when the danger of the ending is glimpsed. Action can be undertaken to engage with the forces that are in collusion with finality; with difficulty and concentrated care, the situation can be retrieved and renewed. Often the very threat of ending can be what animates and develops a relationship. Indeed, the prospect of death is probably the greatest single inspiration of human creativity and passion. The brevity of our presence here is suddenly brought into sharp relief and intensifies our sense of urgency.

On the other hand, endings can be such a relief. When we suffer, we long for it to end. When we are in pain, time crawls. It also darkens and imprisons our imagination; consequently, we are unable to see beyond the suffering that plagues us. Often the greatest gift in such a situation is when someone manages to persuade the eyes of the heart to glimpse the vaguest brightening. Then the imagination takes hope from that, and constructs a path of light out of the darkness. Such endings offer great promise and bring us to the edge of new possibility. They are nascent beginnings. This is one of the fascinating characteristics of consciousness. Unlike the world of matter, in the world of spirit a whole territory that has lain fallow can become a fertile area of new potential and creativity. Time behaves differently in the domain of spirit.

Experience has its own secret structuring. Endings are natural. Often what alarms us as an ending can in fact be the opening of a new journey—a new beginning that we could never have anticipated; one that engages forgotten parts of the heart. Due to the current overlay of therapy terminology in our language, everyone now seems to wish for "closure." This word is unfortunate; it is not faithful to the open-ended rhythm of experience. Creatures made of clay with porous skin and porous minds are quite incapable of the hermetic sealing that the strategy of "closure" seems to imply. The word *completion* is a truer word. Each experience has within it a dynamic of unfolding and a narrative of emergence. Oscar Wilde once said, "The supreme vice is shallowness. Whatever is realized is right." When a person manages to trust experience and be open to it, the experience finds its own way to realization. Though such an ending may be awkward and painful, there is a sense of wholesomeness and authenticity about it. Then the heart will gradually find that this stage has run its course and the ending is substantial and true. Eventually the person emerges with a deeper sense of freedom, certainty, and integration.

The nature of calendar time is linear; it is made up of durations that begin and end. The Celtic imagination always sensed that beneath time there was eternal depth. This offers us a completely different way of relating to time. It relieves time of the finality of ending. While something may come to an ending on the surface of time, its presence, meaning, and effect continue to be held and integrated into the eternal. This is how spirit unfolds and deepens. In this sense, eternal time is intimate; it is where the unfolding narrative of individual life is gathered and woven. Eternal life is eternal memory; therefore, it becomes possible to imagine a realm beyond endings where all that has unfolded is not canceled or lost, but where the spirit-depths of it are already arriving home.

AT THE END OF THE YEAR

The particular mind of the ocean
Filling the coastline's longing
With such brief harvest
Of elegant, vanishing waves
Is like the mind of time
Opening us shapes of days.

As this year draws to its end,
We give thanks for the gifts it brought
And how they became inlaid within
Where neither time nor tide can touch them.

The days when the veil lifted
And the soul could see delight;
When a quiver caressed the heart
In the sheer exuberance of being here.

Surprises that came awake
In forgotten corners of old fields
Where expectation seemed to have quenched.

The slow, brooding times
When all was awkward
And the wave in the mind
Pierced every sore with salt.

The darkened days that stopped
The confidence of the dawn.

Days when beloved faces shone brighter
With light from beyond themselves;
And from the granite of some secret sorrow
A stream of buried tears loosened.

We bless this year for all we learned,
For all we loved and lost
And for the quiet way it brought us
Nearer to our invisible destination.

The Inner History of a Day

No one knew the name of this day;
Born quietly from deepest night,
It hid its face in light,
Demanded nothing for itself,
Opened out to offer each of us
A field of brightness that traveled ahead,
Providing in time, ground to hold our footsteps
And the light of thought to show the way.

The mind of the day draws no attention;
It dwells within the silence with elegance
To create a space for all our words,
Drawing us to listen inward and outward.

We seldom notice how each day is a holy place
Where the eucharist of the ordinary happens,
Transforming our broken fragments
Into an eternal continuity that keeps us.

Somewhere in us a dignity presides
That is more gracious than the smallness
That fuels us with fear and force,
A dignity that trusts the form a day takes.

So at the end of this day, we give thanks
For being betrothed to the unknown
And for the secret work
Through which the mind of the day
And wisdom of the soul become one.

As you huddle around the torn silence,
Each by this lonely deed exiled
To a solitary confinement of soul,
May some small glow from what has been lost
Return like the kindness of candlelight.

As your eyes strain to sift
This sudden wall of dark
And no one can say why
In such a forsaken, secret way,
This death was sent for . . .
May one of the lovely hours
Of memory return
Like a field of ease
Among these graveled days.

May the Angel of Wisdom
Enter this ruin of absence
And guide your minds
To receive this bitter chalice
So that you do not damage yourselves
By attending only at the hungry altar
Of regret and anger and guilt.

May you be given some inkling
That there could be something else at work
And that what to you now seems
Dark, destructive, and forlorn,

Might be a destiny that looks different
From inside the eternal script.

May vision be granted to you
To see this with the eyes of providence.
May your loss become a sanctuary
Where new presence will dwell
To refine and enrich
The rest of your life
With courage and compassion.

And may your lost loved one
Enter into the beauty of eternal tranquillity,
In that place where there is no more sorrow
Or separation or mourning or tears.

FOR BROKEN TRUST

Sometimes there is an invisible raven
That will fly low to pierce the shell of trust
When it has been brought near to ground.

When he strikes, he breaks the faith of years
That had built quietly through the seasons
In the rhythm of tried and tested experience.

With one strike, the shelter is down
And the black yoke of truth turned false
Would poison the garden of memory.

Now the heart's dream turns to requiem,
Offering itself a poultice of tears
To cleanse from loss what cannot be lost.

Through all the raw and awkward days,
Dignity will hold the heart to grace
Lest it squander its dream on a ghost.

Often torn ground is ideal for seed
That can root disappointment deep enough
To yield a harvest that cannot wither:

A deeper light to anoint the eyes,
Passion that opens wings in the heart,
A subtle radiance of countenance:
The soul ready for its true other.

FOR THE BREAKUP OF A RELATIONSHIP

Now you endeavor
To gather yourself
And withdraw in slow
Animal woundedness
From love turned sour and ungentle.

When we love, the depth in us
Trusts itself forward until
The empty space between
Becomes gradually woven
Into an embrace where longing
Can close its weary eyes.

Love can seldom end clean;
For all the tissue is torn
And each lover turned stranger
Is dropped into a ruin of distance
Where emptiness is young and fierce.

Time becomes strange and slipshod;
It mixes memories that felt
The kiss of the eternal
With the blistering hurt of now.

Unknown to themselves,
Certain small things
Touch nerve-lines to the heart
And bring back with color and force
All that is utterly lost.

This is the time to be slow,
Lie low to the wall
Until the bitter weather passes.

Try, as best you can, not to let
The wire brush of doubt
Scrape from your heart
All sense of yourself
And your hesitant light.

If you remain generous,
Time will come good;
And you will find your feet
Again on fresh pastures of promise,
Where the air will be kind
And blushed with beginning.

This is where your life has arrived,
After all the years of effort and toil;
Look back with graciousness and thanks
On all your great and quiet achievements.

You stand on the shore of new invitation
To open your life to what is left undone;
Let your heart enjoy a different rhythm
When drawn to the wonder of other horizons.

Have the courage for a new approach to time;
Allow it to slow until you find freedom
To draw alongside the mystery you hold
And befriend your own beauty of soul.

Now is the time to enjoy your heart's desire,
To live the dreams you've waited for,
To awaken the depths beyond your work
And enter into your infinite source.

FOR SOMEONE AWAKENING TO THE
TRAUMA OF HIS OR HER PAST

For everything under the sun there is a time.
This is the season of your awkward harvesting,
When pain takes you where you would rather
       not go,

Through the white curtain of yesterdays to a place
You had forgotten you knew from the inside out;
And a time when that bitter tree was planted

That has grown always invisibly beside you
And whose branches your awakened hands
Now long to disentangle from your heart.

You are coming to see how your looking often
       darkened
When you should have felt safe enough to fall
       toward love,
How deep down your eyes were always owned by
       something

That faced them through a dark fester of thorns
Converting whoever came into a further figure of
       the wrong;
You could only see what touched you as already
       torn.

Now the act of seeing begins your work of
       mourning.

And your memory is ready to show you everything,
Having waited all these years for you to return and
know.

Only you know where the casket of pain is interred.
You will have to scrape through all the layers of
covering
And according to your readiness, everything will
open.

May you be blessed with a wise and compassionate
guide
Who can accompany you through the fear and grief
Until your heart has wept its way to your true self.

As your tears fall over that wounded place,
May they wash away your hurt and free your heart.
May your forgiveness still the hunger of the wound

So that for the first time you can walk away from
that place,
Reunited with your banished heart, now healed and
freed,
And feel the clear, free air bless your new face.

On the Death of the Beloved

Though we need to weep your loss,
You dwell in that safe place in our hearts
Where no storm or night or pain can reach you.

Your love was like the dawn
Brightening over our lives,
Awakening beneath the dark
A further adventure of color.

The sound of your voice
Found for us
A new music
That brightened everything.

Whatever you enfolded in your gaze
Quickened in the joy of its being;
You placed smiles like flowers
On the altar of the heart.
Your mind always sparkled
With wonder at things.

Though your days here were brief,
Your spirit was alive, awake, complete.

We look toward each other no longer
From the old distance of our names;
Now you dwell inside the rhythm of breath,
As close to us as we are to ourselves.

Though we cannot see you with outward eyes,
We know our soul's gaze is upon your face,
Smiling back at us from within everything
To which we bring our best refinement.

Let us not look for you only in memory,
Where we would grow lonely without you.
You would want us to find you in presence,
Beside us when beauty brightens,
When kindness glows
And music echoes eternal tones.

When orchids brighten the earth,
Darkest winter has turned to spring;
May this dark grief flower with hope
In every heart that loves you.

May you continue to inspire us:
To enter each day with a generous heart.
To serve the call of courage and love
Until we see your beautiful face again
In that land where there is no more separation,
Where all tears will be wiped from our mind,
And where we will never lose you again.

Though its way is to strike
In a dumb rhythm,
Stroke upon stroke,
As though the heart
Were an anvil,
The hurt you sent
Had a mind of its own.

Something in you knew
Exactly how to shape it,
To hit the target,
Slipping into the heart
Through some wound-window
Left open since childhood.

While it struck outside,
It burrowed inside,
Made tunnels through
Every ground of confidence.
For days, it would lie still
Until a thought would start it.

Meanwhile, you forgot,
Went on with things
And never even knew
How that perfect
Shape of hurt
Still continued to work.

Now a new kindness
Seems to have entered time
And I can see how that hurt
Has schooled my heart
In a compassion I would
Otherwise have never learned.

Somehow now
I have begun to glimpse
The unexpected fruit
Your dark gift had planted
And I thank you
For your unknown work.

After a Destructive Encounter

Now that you have entered with an open heart
Into a complex and fragile situation,
Hoping with patience and respect
To tread softly over sore ground in order
That somewhere beneath the raw estrangement
Some fresh spring of healing might be coaxed
To release the grace for a new journey
Beyond repetition and judgment,
And have achieved nothing of that,
But emerged helpless, and with added hurt . . .

Withdraw for a while into your own tranquillity,
Loosen from your heart the new fester.
Free yourself of the wounded gaze
That is not yet able to see you.
Recognize your responsibility for the past.
Don't allow your sense of yourself to wilt.
Draw deep from your own dignity.
Temper your expectation to the other's limits,
And take your time carefully,
Learning that there is a time for everything
And for healing too,
But that now is not that time . . . yet.

Now is the time to free the heart,
Let all intentions and worries stop,
Free the joy inside the self,
Awaken to the wonder of your life.

Open your eyes and see the friends
Whose hearts recognize your face as kin,
Those whose kindness watchful and near,
Encourages you to live everything here.

See the gifts the years have given,
Things your effort could never earn,
The health to enjoy who you want to be
And the mind to mirror mystery.

FOR LOST FRIENDS

As twilight makes a rainbow robe
From the concealed colors of day
In order for time to stay alive
Within the dark weight of night,
May we lose no one we love
From the shelter of our hearts.

When we love another heart
And allow it to love us,
We journey deep below time
Into that eternal weave
Where nothing unravels.

May we have the grace to see
Despite the hurt of rupture,
The searing of anger,
And the empty disappointment,
That whoever we have loved,
Such love can never quench.

Though a door may have closed,
Closed between us,
May we be able to view
Our lost friends with eyes
Wise with calming grace;
Forgive them the damage
We were left to inherit;

Free ourselves from the chains
Of forlorn resentment;
Bring warmth again to
Where the heart has frozen
In order that beyond the walls
Of our cherished hurt
And chosen distance
We may be able to
Celebrate the gifts they brought,
Learn and grow from the pain,
And prosper into difference,
Wishing them the peace
Where spirit can summon
Beauty from wounded space.

I pray that you will have the blessing
Of being consoled and sure about your death.

May you know in your soul
There is no need to be afraid.

When your time comes, may you have
Every blessing and strength you need.

May there be a beautiful welcome for you
In the home you are going to.

You are not going somewhere strange,
Merely back to the home you have never left.

May you live with compassion
And transfigure everything
Negative within and about you.

When you come to die,
May it be after a long life.

May you be tranquil
Among those who care for you.

May your going be sheltered
And your welcome assured.

May your soul smile
In the embrace
Of your Anam Cara.

For the Dying

May death come gently toward you,
Leaving you time to make your way
Through the cold embrace of fear
To the place of inner tranquillity.

May death arrive only after a long life
To find you at home among your own
With every comfort and care you require.

May your leave-taking be gracious,
Enabling you to hold dignity
Through awkwardness and illness.

May you see the reflection
Of your life's kindness and beauty
In all the tears that fall for you.

As your eyes focus on each face,
May your soul take its imprint,
Drawing each image within
As companions for the journey.

May you find for each one you love
A different locket of jeweled words
To be worn around the heart
To warm your absence.

May someone who knows and loves
The complex village of your heart
Be there to echo you back to yourself
And create a sure word-raft
To carry you to the further shore.

May your spirit feel
The surge of true delight
When the veil of the visible
Is raised, and you glimpse again
The living faces
Of departed family and friends.

May there be some beautiful surprise
Waiting for you inside death,
Something you never knew or felt,
Which with one simple touch,

Absolves you of all loneliness and loss,
As you quicken within the embrace
For which your soul was eternally made.

May your heart be speechless
At the sight of the truth
Of all belief had hoped,
Your heart breathless
In the light and lightness
Where each and everything
Is at last its true self

Within that serene belonging
That dwells beside us
On the other side
Of what we see.

As light departs to let the earth be one with night,
Silence deepens in the mind, and thoughts grow
    slow;
The basket of twilight brims over with colors
Gathered from within the secret meadows of the day
And offered like blessings to the gathering Tenebrae.

After the day's frenzy, may the heart grow still,
Gracious in thought for all the day brought,
Surprises that dawn could never have dreamed:
The blue silence that came to still the mind,
The quiver of mystery at the edge of a glimpse,
The golden echoes of worlds behind voices.

Tense faces unable to hide what gripped the heart,
The abrupt cut of a glance or a word that hurt,
The flame of longing that distance darkened,
Bouquets of memory gathered on the heart's altar,
The thorns of absence in the rose of dream.

And the whole while the unknown underworld
Of the mind, turning slowly, in its secret orbit.
May the blessing of sleep bring refreshment and
    release
And the Angel of the moon call the rivers of dream
To soften the hardened earth of the outside life,
Disentangle from the trapped nets the hurt and
    sorrow,
And awaken the young soul for the new tomorrow.

To Retrieve the Lost Art of Blessing

STRUCTURES OF KINDNESS

There is a kindness that dwells deep down in things; it presides everywhere, often in the places we least expect. The world can be harsh and negative, but if we remain generous and patient, kindness inevitably reveals itself. Something deep in the human soul seems to depend on the presence of kindness; something instinctive in us expects it, and once we sense it we are able to trust and open ourselves. Here in Conamara, the mountains are terse and dark; left to themselves they would make for a brooding atmosphere. However, everywhere around and in between there are lakes. The surface of these lakes takes on the variations of the surrounding light to create subtle diffusions of color. Thus their presence qualifies the whole landscape with a sense of warmth and imagination. If we did not feel that some ultimate kindness holds sway, we would feel like outsiders confronted on every side by a world toward which we could make no real bridges.

The word *kindness* has a gentle sound that seems to echo the presence of compassionate goodness. When someone is kind to you, you feel understood and seen. There is no judgment or harsh perception directed toward you.

Kindness has gracious eyes; it is not small-minded or competitive; it wants nothing back for itself. Kindness strikes a resonance with the depths of your own heart; it also suggests that your vulnerability, though somehow exposed, is not taken advantage of; rather, it has become an occasion for dignity and empathy. Kindness casts a different light, an evening light that has the depth of color and patience to illuminate what is complex and rich in difference.

Despite all the darkness, human hope is based on the instinct that at the deepest level of reality some intimate kindness holds sway. This is the heart of blessing. To believe in blessing is to believe that our being here, our very presence in the world, is itself the first gift, the primal blessing. As Rilke says: *Hier zu sein ist so viel*—to be here is immense. Nowhere does the silence of the infinite lean so intensely as around the form of a newly born infant. Once we arrive, we enter into the inheritance of everything that has preceded us; we become heirs to the world. To be born is to be chosen. To be created and come to birth is to be blessed. Some primal kindness chose us and brought us through the forest of dreaming until we could emerge into the clearance of individuality, with a path of life opening before us through the world.

The beginning often holds the clue to everything that follows. Given the nature of our beginning, it is no wonder that our hearts are imbued with longing for beauty, meaning, order, creativity, compassion, and love. We approach the world with this roster of longings and expect that in some way the world will respond and confirm our desire. Our longing knows it cannot force the fulfillment of its desire; yet it does instinctively expect that primal benevolence to respond to it. This is the threshold where blessing comes alive.

WE LIVE ON THE SHORELINE OF THE INVISIBLE

The beauty of the world is the first witness to blessing. In a land without blessing, no beauty could dwell.

The eye adores the visible world. Once it opens, it is already the guest at an unending feast of vision: so much difference clothed in such diverse colors, the sheer range of presence suggested in different intensities of surface, the fecund nearness and the enigmatic distance. For the exploring eye there could be no dream greater than the world that is. The human eye falls in love with the enthralling plenitude of the visible. This fascination is addictive; then almost immediately our amnesia in relation to the invisible sets in. We live in this world as if it had always been our reality and will continue to be. However, when we think about it, we recognize that invisible light does accompany a new infant into the world. We also notice, at the other end, how the shadows of old age are lit more and more from the invisible world. Yet in our day-to-day lives, we continually fail to recognize the invisible light that renders the whole visible world luminous. This light casts no shadow; or perhaps we could invert the usual priority we give to the visible and say that the actual fabric and substance of the visible world is in fact the shadow that this invisible light casts.

Fixated on the visible, we forget that the decisive presences in our lives—soul, mind, thought, love, meaning, time, and life itself—are all invisible. No surgeon has ever opened a brain to discover crevices full of thoughts. And yet our thought determines who we think we are, who we think others are, and how we consider the world to be. We are not the masters of our own reality; granted, we do choose the lenses through which we see the world, yet the shape and color of these lenses are offered to us from the primal benevolence of the unseen world. Everything that is here has had its origin there. The invisible is the parent of the visible.

Before time began the invisible world rested in the eternal. With the creation of our world, time and space began. Every stone, bush, raindrop, star, mountain, and flower has its origin in the invisible world. That is where the first sighting of each of us occurred. We emerged from the folds of time, each an intense mixture of visible and invisible. Our eyes cannot see this world. Our hearts are usually too encumbered to navigate it, our minds too darkened to decipher it. As the Bible says: "Now we see through a glass darkly." Yet it is exactly on this threshold between visible and invisible that our most creative conflicts and challenges come alive. Each new beginning, each new difficulty always finds us on that frontier. And this is exactly why we reach for blessing. In our confusion, fear, and uncertainty we call upon the invisible structures of original kindness to come to our assistance and open pathways of possibility by refreshing and activating in us our invisible potential. When we bless, we work from a place of inner vision, clearer than our hearts, brighter than our minds. Blessing is the art of harvesting the wisdom of the invisible world. From day to day it offers us new gifts.

THE WONDER AND STRANGENESS OF A DAY

Each new day is a path of wonder, a different invitation. Days are where our lives gradually become visible.

Often it seems that we have to undertake the longest journey to arrive at what has been nearest all along. Mornings rarely find us so astounded at the new day that we are unable to decide between adventures. We take on days with the same conditioned reflex with which we wash and put on our clothes each morning. If we could be mindful of how short our time is, we might learn how precious each day is. There are people who will never forget today.

A man awakes this morning beset by an old emptiness that has gnawed for years. By now he is adept at managing it. He accommodates himself to another day; instinctively, he sets the compass of his mind. Later in the morning, at work, he receives a call from a woman he once knew. He had never forgotten her. He always sensed that she might have had the measure of his emptiness. Now, out of the blue, she is wondering if they might meet for dinner. As he puts down the phone, he imagines he can hear a door opening—and senses that things may never be the same again.

Somewhere else a woman awakes beside her husband; she already feels weary at the prospect of the morning's work and the rest of the day minding young children. But she stops herself, coaxes her heart to realize that things are actually great. The relationship has deepened in the last while, the awkwardness with their eldest son has calmed, and the money situation has improved significantly. She gets up, goes to take her shower. At this stage she is even singing quietly to herself. She does her routine breast check and finds the lump. An abyss opens. She will never forget this day.

Meanwhile, we dodder through our days as if they were our surest belongings. No day belongs to us. Each day is a gift. Tragically, it is often only when we are about to lose a thing that the scales fall from our eyes, but it is usually too late. On its way toward us, destiny travels silently, until it arrives. Then something we had never expected becomes loud around us. Time is where eternity unfolds. The contemplative tradition has always recognized the morning as the time to recognize the new day with a sense of creative expectation and openheartedness.

TO RECEIVE EACH DAY AS AN INVITATION

One night recently I visited our family farm. A calf had just been born. It had just slumped to earth in a wet, steaming mass. At midnight I went out to look at the cow again; by this time she had licked her new calf dry and he had sucked his first milk. Everything was mild and gentle, illuminated by the moon's mint light. What a beautiful night it was to arrive on earth. Even if this newborn were a genius, it could never possibly imagine the surprise of the world that was waiting when the dawn would break in a miracle of color illuminating the personality of mountains, river, and sky.

The liturgy of dawn signals the wonder of the arriving day. The magic of darkness breaking through into color and light is such a promise of invitation and possibility. No wonder we always associate the hope and urgency of new beginning with the dawn. Each day is the field of brightness where the invitation of our life unfolds. A new day is an intricate and subtle matrix; written into its mystery are the happenings sent to awaken and challenge us.

No day is ever the same, and no day stands still; each one moves through a different territory, awakening new beginnings. A day moves forward in moments, and once a moment has flickered into life, it vanishes and is replaced by the next. It is fascinating that this is where we live, within an emerging lacework that continuously unravels. Often a fleeting moment can hold a whole sequence of the future in distilled form: that unprepared second when you looked in a parent's eye and saw death already beginning to loom. Or the second you noticed a softening in someone's voice and you knew that a friendship was beginning. Or catching your partner's gaze upon you and knowing the love that surrounded you. Each day is seeded with recognitions.

The writing life is a wonderful metaphor for this. The writer goes to his desk each morning to meet the empty white page. As he settles himself, he is preparing for visitation and voyage. His memory, longing, and craft set the frame for what might emerge. He has no idea what will come. Yet despite his limitations, his creative work will find its own direction to form. Each of us is an artist of our days; the greater our integrity and awareness, the more original and creative our time will become.

TO CROSS THE THRESHOLDS WORTHILY: WHEN A GREAT MOMENT KNOCKS ON THE DOOR OF YOUR HEART

It remains the dream of every life to realize itself, to reach out and lift oneself up to greater heights. A life that continues to remain on the safe side of its own habits and repetitions, that never engages with the risk of its own possibility, remains an unlived life. There is within each heart a hidden voice that calls out for freedom and creativity. We often linger for years in spaces that are too small and shabby for the grandeur of our spirit. Yet experience always remains faithful to us. If lived truthfully and generously, it will always guide us toward the real pastures.

Looking back along a life's journey, you come to see how each of the central phases of your life began at a decisive threshold where you left one way of being and entered another. A threshold is not simply an accidental line that happens to separate one region from another. It is an intense frontier that divides a world of feeling from another. Often a threshold becomes clearly visible only once you have crossed it. Crossing can often mean the total loss of all you enjoyed while on the other side; it becomes a dividing line between the past and the future. More often than not, the reason you cannot return to where you were is that you have changed; you are no longer the one who crossed over. It is interesting that when Jesus cured the blind man, he instructed him not to go back into the village. Having crossed the threshold into vision, his life was no longer to be lived in the constricted mode of blindness; new vision meant new pastures.

Today many people describe themselves as "being in transition." In a culture governed by speed, this is to be expected, for the exterior rate of change is relentless. This "transition" can refer to relationships, work, and location; or more significantly, to the inner life and way of viewing the world. Yet the word *transition* seems to be pale, functional, almost inadequate and impersonal, and does not have the same intensity or psychic weight as perhaps the word *threshold* evokes. The word *threshold* was related to the word *thresh*, which was the separation of the grain from the husk or straw when oats were flailed. It also includes the notions of *entrance, crossing, border,* and *beginning.* To cross a threshold is to leave behind the husk and arrive at the grain.

THE LOSS OF RITUAL LEAVES US NAKED IN OUR RITES OF PASSAGE

A threshold is a significant frontier where experience banks up; there is intense concrescence. It is a place of great transformation. Some of the most powerful thresholds divide worlds from each other: life in the womb from birth, childhood from adolescence, adulthood from middle age, old age from death. And on each side there is a different geography of feeling, thinking, and being. The crossing of a threshold is in effect a rite of passage.

Our culture has little to offer us for our crossings. Never was there such talk of communication or such technology to facilitate it. Yet at the heart of our newfound wealth and progress there is a gaping emptiness, and we are haunted by loneliness. While we seem to have progressed to become experts in so many things—multiplying and acquiring stuff we neither need nor truly want—we have unlearned the grace of presence and belonging. With the demise of religion, many people are left stranded in a chasm of emptiness and doubt; without rituals to recognize, celebrate, or negotiate the vital thresholds of people's lives, the key crossings pass by, undistinguished from the mundane, everyday rituals of life. This is where we need to retrieve and reawaken our capacity for blessing. If we approach our decisive thresholds with reverence and attention, the crossing will bring us more than we could ever have hoped for. This is where blessing invokes and awakens every gift the crossing has to offer. In our present ritual poverty, the Celtic tradition has much to offer us.

THE CELTIC SENSE OF TIME AS CREATIVE OCCASION

Always, when my father left home to go to work in the fields or to go to town, the last thing he did as he walked out the door was to turn back toward us in the kitchen and inhale a full explicit breath. I had never really thought about this image from childhood until I started writing this book. And it seems that what he was doing as he left was inhaling the spirit of his loved ones to nourish and protect his journey, coming back to take for himself a blessing-breath.

We know that there will be a time when a certain farewell will be the last. In French, *au revoir* and in German *Auf wiedersehen* both explicitly state the wish that we might be seen again. In Irish, we say *slan leat* or *go dte tu slan*: "safety be with you," or "may you go safely." Our forms of greeting express joy and delight that the person is still there. In German, the surprise is almost palpable: *Da bist Du* . . . "there you are." Or *Gruss Dich* "greetings to you." In Irish we say, *Dia Dhuit*, "God to you," and the response is, *Dia 's Muire Dhuit*, "God and Mary to you." Beyond the courtesy of convention, this manner of words suggests that your being there still is an act of divine kindness. Blessing always shores up the heart against the ravages of time; this is wonderfully expressed in Conamara when one puts on a new garment: *Go maire tu agus go gcaithe tu e agus go gcaithe tu seacht gcinn nios fearr na e*: "May you live and may you wear it and may you wear seven more even better than it." Blessing is intended to strengthen human presence, and it often harnesses the energy of nature to affect this.

In the Celtic world there is a great tradition of blessing. Because it was primarily an oral tradition, the blessings were learned by heart and handed on from one generation to the next. There are blessings for every possible occasion. The Celtic mind had a refined sense of occasion.

The human mind cannot encompass the full weight of time. We break time up into divisions we can manage. But the word *occasion* suggests a period of special time when something of significance unfolds. In Western culture, occasion is now mere social occasion. Yet for the person who lives time consciously, there is a continuous undertow of possibility always at work. Accordingly, it is received and appreciated as continuous occasions of invitation. To live like this is to experience time as a constant invitation to growth—to become more than you have been, to transform loss into presence, and to allow what is false to fall away. At the gates of time, blessing waits to usher toward us the grace we need.

TO BLESS WITH HOLY WATER

While blessing is an act of the senses expressed in word and gesture, the source and the destination of blessing remain invisible. Perhaps this is why water has always been used as a vehicle of blessing. In elemental terms, water stands midway between the physicality of earth and fire and the unseen air. Water is colorless, odorless, and transparent; it has a huge affinity with the unseen and yet achieves a tentative and sometimes forceful visibility. The origin of water retains its secrecy; the source is always out of human view. Crucially water is the mother and vehicle of life. The human body is over eighty percent water, and the fertility of the earth is directly dependent on it. Given this metaphoric range, water is the ideal liturgical vehicle to confer blessing.

In the Christian tradition, water is always blessed before use; this is understood to infuse the water with the energy of the Holy Spirit, the carrier of the Trinity. Holy water is used in the sacraments to bless and confer transformation. Before the coffin is lowered, the grave is blessed. Holy water is often sprinkled at night for the souls in purgatory, and also for exiles and to protect those traveling. It is also often carried in cars to protect from accident and danger. Furthermore, it is held to be powerful in protecting us from evil; no such spirit would enter a circle of holy water.

Traditionally in Ireland, the act of blessing was not separate from daily life. When baking bread, a woman would put the sign of the cross on the dough with a knife. Each year on St. Bridget's Eve, my uncle always made a little timber cross and nailed it to the ceiling to protect our home for the next year. On this night it is also customary to leave a piece of cloth out overnight, then take it in the next morning dripping with dew. This was the Brath Bride; it brings luck and blessing for the year. On May morning—Beltane—people often wash their faces in the morning dew for healing and health. On St. John's night, some of the fire is put out along the fields of the farm to protect it. On February 3, the feast day of Saint Blaise, people have their throats blessed. February 2 is the feast of Candlemas. On this day wax candles are brought to the church to be blessed. It is very important to have these blessed candles in the house. Anytime during the year when there is trouble the blessed candle is lit. Furthermore, inanimate objects when blessed can become vehicles of grace and protection; this includes medals, scapulars, rosaries, and crucifixes.

In all these modes of blessing the objects are seen to

take on the infusion of sacred power, and long after the occasion of blessing has passed the blessed object still retains
its protective power. There is certain poignancy in this belief that blessing can enter the silence and privacy of the
object and continue to dwell there. It changes the nature of
the object; it is no longer simply itself. Now it is a live sanctuary from which the divine light and protection proceed.
Be it water, metal, fire, or candle: each can be penetrated
and benevolently permeated by the breath of blessing.
These practices also recognize how precarious the work of
day-to-day living can be: there can be danger or darkness
anywhere. Habitual time can turn in a second, and suddenly some unforeseen suffering is taking up tenancy in
one's life. These blessing objects are meant to become active
at these frontier apertures where one could be damaged.

A BLESSING IS A PROTECTIVE CIRCLE OF LIGHT

What is a blessing? A blessing is a circle of light drawn
around a person to protect, heal, and strengthen. Life is a
constant flow of emergence. The beauty of blessing is its
belief that it can affect what unfolds.

To be in the world is to be distant from the homeland
of wholeness. We are confined by limitation and difficulty.
When we bless, we are enabled somehow to go beyond our
present frontiers and reach into the source. A blessing
awakens future wholeness. We use the word *foreshadow* for
the imperfect representation of something that is yet to
come. We could say that a blessing "forebrightens" the way.

When a blessing is invoked, a window opens in eternal time.

The word *blessing* comes from the Old English: *Blêtsian, blêdsian, blœdsian.* As intimated in the sound of *blêdsian* it means "to sanctify or consecrate with blood." It is interesting that though the word *blessing* sounds abstract, a thing of the word and the air, in its original meaning it was vitally connected to the life force. In ancient traditions blood was life; it connected the earthly, the human, and the divine. To bless also means to invoke divine favor upon.

We never see the script of our lives; nor do we know what is coming toward us, or why our life takes on this particular shape or sequence. A blessing is different from a greeting, a hug, a salute, or an affirmation; it opens a different door in human encounter. One enters into the forecourt of the soul, the source of intimacy and the compass of destiny.

Our longing for the eternal kindles our imagination to bless. Regardless of how we configure the eternal, the human heart continues to dream of a state of wholeness, a place where everything comes together, where loss will be made good, where blindness will transform into vision, where damage will be made whole, where the clenched question will open in the house of surprise, where the travails of a life's journey will enjoy a homecoming. To invoke a blessing is to call some of that wholeness upon a person now.

There is an implicit wholeness in the human heart; it is a huge treasure house that we draw on every day. Ultimately it is what anchors and guides us. A simple metaphor for this is a physical wound. When you have a wound in your hand, it always heals from the edges; the center is the last place to heal. Clearly it is not the wound that has finally relented and decided to heal itself. Rather it is the surrounding health and wholesomeness of your body that invades the stricken place with healing. The mind of blessing is wise, and it knows that whatever torments or diminishes a person cannot be healed simply from within that diminishment; consequently it addresses the wholeness and draws that light and healing into the diminished area. When someone blesses you, the fruits of healing may surprise you and seem to come from afar. In fact, they are your own natural serenity and sureness awakening and arriving around you.

In my family, our parents always insisted before and after meals, at the rosary, and at the Angelus time that we bless ourselves and say the appropriate prayers. Lately that simple ritual has come back to me with new echoes: Bless yourself. If each of us has the ability to shape and form our lives through our thinking, do we not also have a huge ability to bless our lives?

While we live in the world, we always live in distance. Often the greatest distance is not physical but mental. Maya Angelou has said, "And lovers think quite different thoughts while lying side by side." Often the nature of one's mind is what separates us most from another. There is also the emotional distance when some hurt or wound constructs a wall between friends. In the west of Ireland, we share the interesting phrase: "I have fallen out with someone." Once the bond of kinship and togetherness is broken, you fall out of it; i.e., you fall into distance again. Though distance can have many forms of separation, it need never be spiritual. One can still continue to remain close in spirit to the distanced one.

The beauty of blessing is that it recognizes no barriers—and no distances. All the given frontiers of blockage that separate us can be penetrated by the loving subtlety of blessing. This can often be the key to awakening and creating forgiveness. We often linger in the crippling states of anger and resentment. Hurt is always unfair and unexpected; it can leave a bitter residue that poisons the space between us. Eventually the only way forward is forgiveness. We tend to see forgiveness as the willingness to see beyond what has been done to us; and it is. But the gift of forgiveness is also a gift to us. When we forgive, we free ourselves. No longer do we hang, sore and torn from the injury done to us. Even though it goes against the grain at first, when we practice sending blessing to those who have injured us, forgiveness begins to become possible. It is always amazing to meet someone who has been hurt, and find that they have broken out of the trap of victimhood and managed to bring compassion and forgiveness to the one who wronged them. They have gone beyond the emotional geometry of the situation, beyond reaction, beyond the psychology of it. They have transcended the natural structure of expectation and managed to tap into some deeper flow of destiny that can integrate and overcome the injustice of hurt. They have entered a vision larger than the wounded view from the present situation. In situations you would expect to be wired with hard lines of justified resentment and bitterness, it is always surprising to discover beneath the surface fluent veins of compassion and forgiveness.

"WHILE HE WAS STILL A LONG WAY OFF . . ."

There is no distance in spiritual space. This is what blessing does: it converts distance into spiritual space. It is as though the very idea of blessing was designed for the traveler who is still far from home. Some of the tranquillity and completion of the destination itself sets out to approach and embrace the one who is still a long way off. The approach of blessing is reminiscent of the father who is at the door looking out, awaiting the return of the prodigal son; the lovely phrase is: "While he was still a long way off." On the journey, the pilgrim will have to traverse thresholds that will test every conviction and instinct. It is especially at such thresholds that the plenitude of blessing is needed.

On our farm in the winter, we put the cattle out on the mountains into the winterage. There the grass has been preserved all year. Even in the worst of weather, in frost and snow, the cattle still have fresh fodder. Because the landscape is bleak, there is little shelter. Every so often out there, one notices semicircular walls. The cattle know them well. These are the "sheltering walls" when winds and storms blow up. Similarly, when you invoke a blessing, you are creating a "sheltering wall" of rest and peace around a person. Ultimately, nothing need be deemed negative if embraced rightly. So much depends not on how awkward destiny is, but rather on how openly it is embraced. This is what the "sheltering wall" of blessing can enable.

BLESSING OUR ZONES OF OMISSION

When we look back on our lives, things become clear in a way they never were while they were happening. We see again a situation where someone was being badly treated or bullied, but we remained silent. Perhaps there was a time when something unworthy was beginning, and a simple action from us would have prevented the damage, but we did nothing. At another time perhaps we were part of something that was developing negatively, perhaps in a relationship or at work, and we never had the courage to say how we felt; we simply went along with it. In this way we damaged our integrity and our dignity. It is chastening to look back and see how frequently our silence allowed damage to occur and perhaps shored up something that was cruel, negative. It is easy to feel regretful that we did not stand up clearly and courageously then. But we know that at that time it was hard, maybe impossible, to speak out, and we live with a sense of something unresolved.

Gradually over the years, a parallel life of undone things builds up. The unresolved has a lingering force and it follows us. Because this happens in the unconscious and unknown regions of our hearts, we rarely notice its effect. The undone continues to live near us; sometimes it is more powerful than what we have actually completed. What is finished lets us go free; it becomes truly part of us and is integrated and woven into memory. What remains unfinished continues to dwell in that still hungry and unformed part of the heart that could not realize itself and grow free; these gaps in our integrity stay open and hungry. This is one of the neglected areas that can be reframed by blessing.

WHO CAN BLESS? EVERYONE?

When I was a young priest I had occasion to visit a contemplative community of sisters. An old sister opened the door. Knowing that I was a new priest, she asked for my first blessing. I stood over this contemplative and drew on every resource I knew to invoke the most intimate blessing. As I was completing the blessing, it struck me how ironical this situation was: here was a contemplative who had spent over sixty years of her life navigating the searing silence and darkness of God, yet she was asking a twenty-five-year-old for his blessing. When she stood up I decided to kneel down and ask her for her blessing. She seemed utterly taken aback; she mumbled something and practically ran out of the room. She must never have had such a request for her blessing before. This was a woman who practiced a totally contemplative life, and yet the system made her feel that she could not bless, and, conversely, it made me think I could. This experience led me to question who had the authority and power to bless.

Who has the power to bless? This question is not to be answered simply by the description of one's institutional status or membership. But perhaps there are deeper questions hidden here: What do you bless with? Or where do you bless from? When you bless another, you first gather yourself; you reach below your surface mind and personality, down to the deeper source within you—namely, the soul. Blessing is from soul to soul. And the key to who you are is your soul.

THE SOUL OF BLESSING

How we think determines so much of what happens to us. Sometimes we are unaware of the most powerful truths about ourselves, for instance, that each of us has a soul. We go on with our everyday lives as if we are completely dependent on our own ability, though aware of how frail and limited that can be. The world of spirit is strange; it is subtle and concealed; it will wait for our calling. If you never think of your soul but confine it to some vague region of spiritual fantasy, you squander an infinite energy at the heart of your life. Once you awaken to your soul, you know that you are no longer alone; nor are you at the mercy of your own frailty and limitation. Awakening to your soul, you begin to learn another way of being in the world. The old barriers no longer confine you, the old wounds no longer name you, and the old fears no longer claim you. Not that all of this simply disappears in some new, born-again conversion. A blessing does not erase the difficult nor abolish it; but it does reach deeper to draw out the hidden fruit of the negative. The old patterns do not evaporate, but become transformed under the persuasion of the soul's new affection.

The core of the human is not some psychological cellar that holds the crippled shapes of our woundedness and destructive choices, but the soul, the core self that dovetails into the infinite. Meister Eckhart said: The soul has two faces; one is directed toward your life, the other toward God. Our literal lifeline is this continuity with the infinite. To realize and believe this increases confidence; it can light up every thought, word, and action. Ultimately, thought is the infinite, breathing inside the word. Our grounding in the soul means that regardless of how badly we think of ourselves, there is a wholesomeness in us that no one has ever been able to damage. The intention of friendship, love, and prayer is to allow your heart to enter this inner sanctuary where it can regain its confidence, renew its energy, and quicken with critical and creative vision. The soul is the home of vision.

This is the secret heart of the whole adventure of blessing. It is not the invention of what is not there, nor the glazed-eyed belief that the innocent energy of goodwill can alter what is destructive. Blessing is a more robust and grounded presence; it issues from the confident depth of the hidden self, and its vision and force can transform what is deadlocked, numbed, and inevitable. When you bless someone, you literally call the force of their infinite self into action.

When a blessing is being invoked, time deepens until it becomes a source from which refreshment and encouragement are released. As Yeats says: Feeling I was blessed and that I now too could bless.

Wherever one person takes another into the care of their heart, they have the power to bless. There are things we never do, simply because it never occurs to us that we can do them. To bless someone is to offer a beautiful gift. When we love someone, we turn toward them with our souls. And the soul itself is the source of blessing.

A blessing is a form of grace; it is invisible. Grace is the permanent climate of divine kindness. There are no limits to it; it has no compartments, corners, or breakage in its flow. For the one who believes in it, a blessing can signal the start of a journey of transformation. It belongs to the same realm as the inner life—its effect becomes only indirectly visible in the changed quality of one's experience. Where before gravity and deadness had prevailed, there is now a new sense of animation and lightness. Where there was grief, a new sense of presence comes alive. In the wall of blindness a window of vision opens.

WHEN BLESSINGS FLOW THROUGH THE HANDS . . .

The Bible is full of blessings. They are seen as a communication of life from God. Once the blessing is spoken, it cannot be annulled or recalled. It is often recommended that we should ask for blessing. "Ask advice of every wise person and blessing of every holy one." There is also the tradition in the Bible that a blessing is imparted by laying one's hands on the head of the one being blessed. When one is in sorrow or pain, touch can become the silent language that says everything; it travels deeper than words can. The head is where consciousness is centered; therefore blessing is always a blessing of consciousness. In the sacrament of ordination, the whole force and power of the sacrament is conveyed and actualized through the laying on of hands, essentially through blessing. The force of a blessing can penetrate through and alter the inner configuration of identity. When the gift or need of the individual coincides with the incoming force of the blessing, great change can begin.

Some years ago I had a series of car accidents, one after

another. I began to feel a darkness tightening around me. I realized that I needed to have that shell broken. I knew an old priest who was totally unconventional and deeply holy. I knelt down and he laid his frail hands on my head and blessed me in Latin. Then he put his hands under my arms and raised me up and said, *"Ni tharloidh tada dhuit, anois a mhac"*—"Nothing will happen to you now, son." Immediately I felt that whatever negativity had had me in its sights had been dissuaded.

KINDNESS IS A MODE OF BLESSING

Perhaps we bless one another all the time, without even realizing it. When we show compassion or kindness to another, we are setting blessing in train. There is a way in which an act of kindness becomes an independent luminous thing, a kind of jewel box of light that might conceal itself for days or years, until one day when you are in desperate straits, you notice something on the floor at your feet, you reach for it, and you discover exactly the courage and vision for which you desperately hunger.

Perhaps this is also true of places. When you are in a certain place, great love or kindness happens; it imprints itself on the ether of the place. When we pass there, hungry and needy in spirit, that loving imprint shines on us like an icon. In folk culture one always knew where to go when sorrow darkened the heart. These places can also act like a poultice to take the poison out of the heart's wounds. Rilke recommended that when life became turbulent and troublesome, it was wise to stay close to one simple thing in nature. A friend of mine who had great trouble with her mind told me once that she had brought a stone into her apartment, and when she felt her mind going, she would concentrate on the stone. She said, "There is a fierce sanity in stone."

THE INNER FRIENDS OF THE HEART

It is such a privilege to have people who continue each day to bless us with their love and prayer. These inner friends of the heart confer on us inestimable gifts. In these times of greed and externality, there is such unusual beauty in having friends who practice profound faithfulness to us, praying for us each day without our ever knowing or remembering it. There are often lonesome frontiers we could never endure or cross without the inner sheltering of these friends. It is hard to live a true life that endeavors to be faithful to its own calling and not become haunted by the ghosts of negativity; therefore, it is not a luxury to have such friends; it is necessary.

I have always loved the shy beauty of country people who have quietly made their lives sacred. Their presence has the feel of unaffected authenticity. Theirs is a spirituality that draws no attention to itself; it is more beautiful than most institutional religious decorum or studied spirituality. These people have often lived through great difficulty, but their quiet and subtle lives never saw any need for brash declarations of spirit; rather they exhibited the shyness that is natural to the soul itself.

Much modern spirituality and psychology is full of loneliness. Much of it is the fruit of emptiness; it has not grown naturally from minds conversant with the eros of the earth. It lacks the rhythm and belonging of a true ecology of the heart; it has a hunger at its core that inevitably breeds narcissism and the mechanics of relentless self-observation, whereas the spirituality of country people seems always to issue from a sense of belonging to a deeper, more ultimate order. They see life as an act of creative service and the world as call to full participation. Theirs is a lifestyle infused with blessing. There are blessings for putting down the fire in the morning, blessings before and after meals, blessings for the start of work, blessings for the person who met you, blessings for the gifts a day brought, blessings of acceptance for the untoward elements that arrived, blessings for health, journeys, animals, and the dead. This weave of blessings is a constant activity of what is now called "mindfulness," a recognition of the miracle of being here, on the constant shoreline of pure arrival. These blessings are also an acceptance of the transitory and terminal nature of all gifts that have arrived; they need not have come. It is also recognition that the spaces of home and landscape are the apertures through which divinity emerges to enfold us. The spirituality of the rural mind does not see time as routine or treadmill; time is a far more precious space where crevices open into the infinite, and where the rhythm of the eternal is felt to preside.

I imagine that one of the great storehouses of blessing
is the invisible neighborhood where the dead dwell. Our
friends among the dead now live where time and space are
transfigured. They behold us now in ways they never could
have when they lived beside us on earth. Because they live
near the source of destiny, their blessings for us are accu-
rate and penetrating, offering a divine illumination not
available according to the calculations of the given visible
world. Perhaps one of the surprises of death will be a retro-
spective view of the lives we lived here and to see how our
friends among the dead clothed us in weave after weave of
blessing.

In folk culture, there is a huge power attributed to the
curse. When invoked, a curse could kill someone. If dark in-
tent can travel the negative path to hit its target, should the
bright intention not be as capable of traveling the creative
path to heal the loved one? It is impossible to underesti-
mate the power of the human mind and the forces it can
unleash. It seems that when a person finds himself in ex-
tremis and gathers his mind and calls out, something
comes awake in the highest regions of destiny. Time behaves differently when blessing is invoked.

It was Kierkegaard who said that life must be lived forward, but it can only be understood backward. Most of the time we are unaware of how blessed our lives are. Poets often refer to an occasional poem as a "found poem." In contrast to the usual travails, frustrations, and endless versions through which most poems come to life, this is a poem that practically wrote itself. Perhaps in terms of blessing, we could say the same: there are around our lives "found blessings." Friendship, for instance, is one. Yeats once said, friendship is the only house we have to offer. Without the blessing of friendship, we would never have become who we are. In the climate of love and understanding that friendship provides, we take root and blossom into full human beings. Our friends are the mirrors where we recognize ourselves, and quite often it is their generosity of spirit that has enabled us to grow and flourish. There is also the blessing of health: the ability to see, to hear, to understand, and to celebrate life. The found blessings also include the gifts that we find coming alive in our lives, abilities that sleep in our hearts that we never suspected. There are also the blessings of our discoveries and modest accomplishments. All of these have been given to us; on our own we could never have merited or earned them. The more we recognize our found blessings, the more they increase around us.

On certain birthdays the shape of our unfolding life comes
into clearer view. Because we are netted into the webbing
of each day's chores and duties, we seldom see the shape
our lives have taken. When we look back, we can identify
the key thresholds where the vital happenings of our lives
occurred. These were usually the times when we were confronted with decisions about the paths we wanted to travel.
Perhaps there were seven of these decisive thresholds in
your life up to now. When you look at each threshold, you
see that you had several choices at each point. You could
always choose only one path. In this way the person you
are today is the result of the path you chose. Out of these
choices you have inherited and shaped your chosen life.
This is the life you live now. This is the person you have
become. When you visit these thresholds, you will see
how you chose your life.

　　The interesting question is, What happened to the lives
you once had as options but did not choose? Where do
they dwell? Perhaps your unlived lives run parallel to your
current life and in some subtle way continue to influence
the choices you make. All this might be happening beside
you and in you, yet unknown to you. Maybe these unlived
yet still unfolding lives are the sustenance from which your
chosen life draws. Maybe this is one of the secrets of death:
that you die only when your invisible, unchosen lives have
also fulfilled themselves, so that you bring into the eternal
world not only your one known life but also the unknown,
unchosen lives as well. Maybe your visible life is but the

outer edge of a whole enterprise of creativity and realization in which you are unknowingly involved. This unseen ground of your unfolding in the world is a place that needs blessing and holds the key to the invisible. Blessing strengthens the network of presence you carry through the world.

BLESSING OUR WORLD NOW

Sometimes when we look out, the world seems so dark. War, violence, hunger, and misery seem to abound. This makes us anxious and helpless. What can I do in my private little corner of life that could have any effect on the march of world events? The usual answer is: nothing. We then decide to do what we can for our own, and leave the great events to their domain. Thus, we opt out, and join the largest majority in the world: those who acquiesce. Believing ourselves to be helpless, we hand over all our power to forces and systems outside us that then act in our names; they go on to put their beliefs into action; and ironically these actions are often sinister and destructive. We live in times when the call to full and critically aware citizenship could not be more urgent. We need to rediscover the careless courage, yet devastating simplicity, of the little boy who, in the middle of the numbed multitude, in naive Socratic fashion, blurts out: "But the emperor has no clothes." When spoken, the word of truth can bring down citadels of falsity.

Real presence is the ideal of all true individuation. When we yield to helplessness, we strengthen the hand of those who would destroy. When we choose indifference, we betray our world. Yet the world is not decided by action alone. It is decided more by consciousness and spirit; they are the secret sources of all action and behavior. The spirit of a time is an incredibly subtle, yet hugely powerful force. And it is comprised of the mentality and spirit of all individuals together. Therefore, the way you look at things is not simply a private matter. Your outlook actually and concretely affects what goes on. When you give in to helplessness, you collude with despair and add to it. When you take back your power and choose to see the possibilities for healing and transformation, your creativity awakens and flows to become an active force of renewal and encouragement in the world. In this way, even in your own hidden life, you can become a powerful agent of transformation in a broken, darkened world. There is a huge force field that opens when intention focuses and directs itself toward transformation.

THE INESTIMABLE POWER OF INTENTION

There is incredible power in the mind when it directs its light toward an object. I heard recently of an ongoing experiment in an American university. There is a sealed-off room; in that room there is a coin-flipping machine. All day and all night it flips coins. The results are usually fifty percent heads and fifty percent tails. Nearby there is another room into which people are invited. Each person is asked to make an intention. Which would they prefer? Heads or tails? Having made their choice, they then write it down on a page that is put in a sealed envelope and addressed to the team who conducts the research. The results are astounding. If a person wishes for heads, the machine ends up flipping up to a seventy-five percent majority of heads and vice versa. They found the distance that the power of the intention to affect the outcome held for up to a hundred-and-fifty-mile radius around the experimentation room. Now, if human intention can substantially affect the outcome of something as cold and neutral as the working of a coin-flipping machine, how much more must our human intentions achieve as they relate to one another?

I have also heard of an experiment in meditation. For a certain number of days, some years ago, a group of people made a circle around the city of Washington and meditated continually. Gathered unknown to itself within this circle of loving kindness, Washington changed. The statistics for that period in the city showed a remarkable and unprecedented decrease in violence and crime. The power of intention to bless is not some utopian fantasy; it can be shown factually to effect concrete and transformative action.

We have no idea the effect we actually have on one another. This is where blessing can achieve so much. Blessing as powerful and positive intention can transform situations and people. The force of blessing must be even more powerful when we consider how the intention of blessing corresponds with the deepest desire of reality for creativity, healing, and wholesomeness. Blessing has pure agency because it animates on the deepest threshold between being and becoming; it mines the territories of memory to awaken and draw forth possibilities we cannot even begin to imagine!

I imagine the eyes of Jesus
Were harvest brown,
The light of their gazing
Suffused with the seasons:

The shadow of winter,
The mind of spring,
The blues of summer,
And amber of harvest.

A gaze that is perfect sister
To the kindness that dwells
In his beautiful hands.

The eyes of Jesus gaze on us,
Stirring in the heart's clay
The confidence of seasons
That never lose their way to harvest.

This gaze knows the signature
Of our heartbeat, the first glimmer
From the dawn that dreamed our minds,

The crevices where thoughts grow
Long before the longing in the bone
Sends them toward the mind's eye,

The artistry of the emptiness
That knows to slow the hunger
Of outside things until they weave
Into the twilight side of the heart,

A gaze full of all that is still future
Looking out for us to glimpse
The jeweled light in winter stone,

Quickening the eyes that look at us
To see through to where words
Are blind to say what we would love,

Forever falling softly on our faces,
His gaze plies the soul with light,
Laying down a luminous layer

Beneath our brief and brittle days
Until the appointed dawn comes
Assured and harvest deft

To unravel the last black knot
And we are back home in the house
That we have never left.

Acknowledgments

I tender my gratitude to Martin Downey for his friendship and understanding over long years; Sheila O'Sullivan and Ethel Balfe for their care and companionship; Kim Witherspoon, Alexis Hurley, and all at Inkwell Management; my editor, Trace Murphy, at Random House for his belief in the book and for his courtesy and kindness. Heartfelt appreciation to my great friend Lelia Doolan for reading the text at an early stage and delivering a surgical critique tempered with encouragement; Loretta Roome for her care for the text and her impatience for its ideal form; Wendy Dubit for her careful reading, her warmth of heart, and sharpness of eye; Dr. Gareth Higgins for his critique and his dignified capacity for friendship; Colen Fraser Wishart for the shelter of his monastic soul; Swami Nicholas Roosevelt for all the great voyages; the artist Catherine Clancy, whose spirit and passion open new windows and whose conversations continue to sing in the mind; the poet-farmer Noel Hanlon, whose imagination and love make the world warmer; Professor Laurie Johnson, whose friendship is a treasure; Professor Helen Riess, whose wise and kind presence creates pathways to retrieve what was lost; Caroline and Dan Siegel for our discovery of kinship and affinity; Pat O'Brien for his presence and friendship; David Whyte, my brother at these frontiers; Jacki Lyden for her love and all the doors she opens in the mind; Jennifer Vecchi for her elegant gentleness; Ellen Wingard for the affinity and belonging; Anna Maria Haughian for her love and prayer; Pat Moore for his kindness and seeing; Linda Alvarez, who has just begun to work with me, for her care, kindness and support. To Kristine Fleck for opening such a beautiful, long-sought circle of echo and belonging. And to the circle of my family that shelters, strengthens, and opens the spirit: P. J. Pat, Mary, Dympna, Eilish, Shane, Katie, Triona, and Peter; to my mother, Josie, whose life and love continue to bless us all.

In memory of Gabriel Joyce, whose wild, clear spirit was always a call to true presence. In memory of John Devitt, who often cast his erudite and elegant eye over my writing. I miss his enriching presence, his passion for beauty, intellect, and refinement of spirit. Never expecting death to come so soon, I am lonesome for all the conversations we never had. And finally, in memory of my lovely uncle Pete, our second father, whose heart loved the mountains and whose voice and passion blessed courage and adventure; and my father, Paddy, the holiest man I ever met. His quiet facility for presence altered space, his gentle eyes always in love with the invisible world.

Certain phrases in the text derive from the following sources:

In the Interim Time: "The old is not old enough to have died away and the young is still too young to be born" is from Gramsci.

In "The Eyes of Jesus": "Back home in the house that we have never left" is from Meister Eckhart.

For Citizenship: "Turn anger into anxiety" is from James Hillman; Turn anxiety back into anger" is from Robert Bly.

About the Author

JOHN O'DONOHUE is the author of several books, including, most recently, *Beauty*, and the international bestsellers *Anam Cara* and *Eternal Echoes*, as well as two collections of poetry, *Echoes of Memory* and *Conamara Blues*. He lives in Ireland and frequently travels to the United States to give lectures and conduct workshops.